COLLECTING OLD GOLFING CLUBS

Alick A. Watt

Alick A. Watt

Published by
A. A. Watt & Son
6, Musgrove Gardens
Alton, Hants GU34 2EQ
1st Impression 1985

Artwork, Graphics and Design
Jim Oswald

ISBN 0 9510923 0 8

Typeset by
R D Composition Ltd,
1a Park Circus Place, Glasgow G3 6AH
Printed by
McNaughtan & Sinclair Ltd,
Rosyth Road, Polmadie Industrial Estate, Glasgow G5 0XX

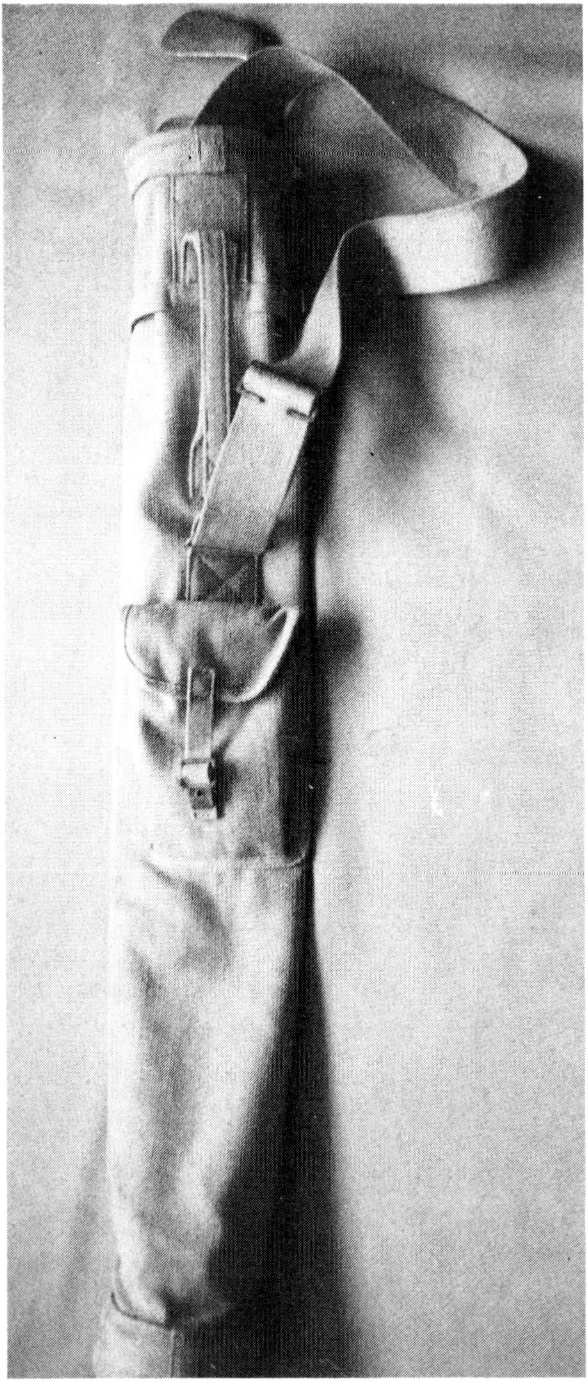

Left – A collector's piece. A bag made from surplus army webbing circa 1920.

ACKNOWLEDGEMENTS

I WOULD like to express my thanks to the undermentioned for their help and advice in producing this book.

Mr Morris Anderson
Mr Eric Auchterlonie
Mr Jim Horsfield
Mr Laurie Auchterlonie
Mr George Collie
Mr Norman Collie
Mr George Colville D.C.M.
Mr I. T. Henderson C.B.E.
Mr Percy Huggins
Mr Pat Garrow
Mr James Watt (Dirleton)
Mr John Letters O.B.E.
Mr R. G. Sams (J. B. Halley & Co. Ltd.)
Mr S. Baxter (P. G. Allday & Co. Ltd.)
Mr D. I. Stirk
Mr Morton Olman
Mr Malcolm Campbell (Editor Golf Monthly)
The Staff of Golf Monthly

Also my wife Betty for the hours she spent over the typewriter and the many other friends who encouraged me to complete the work.

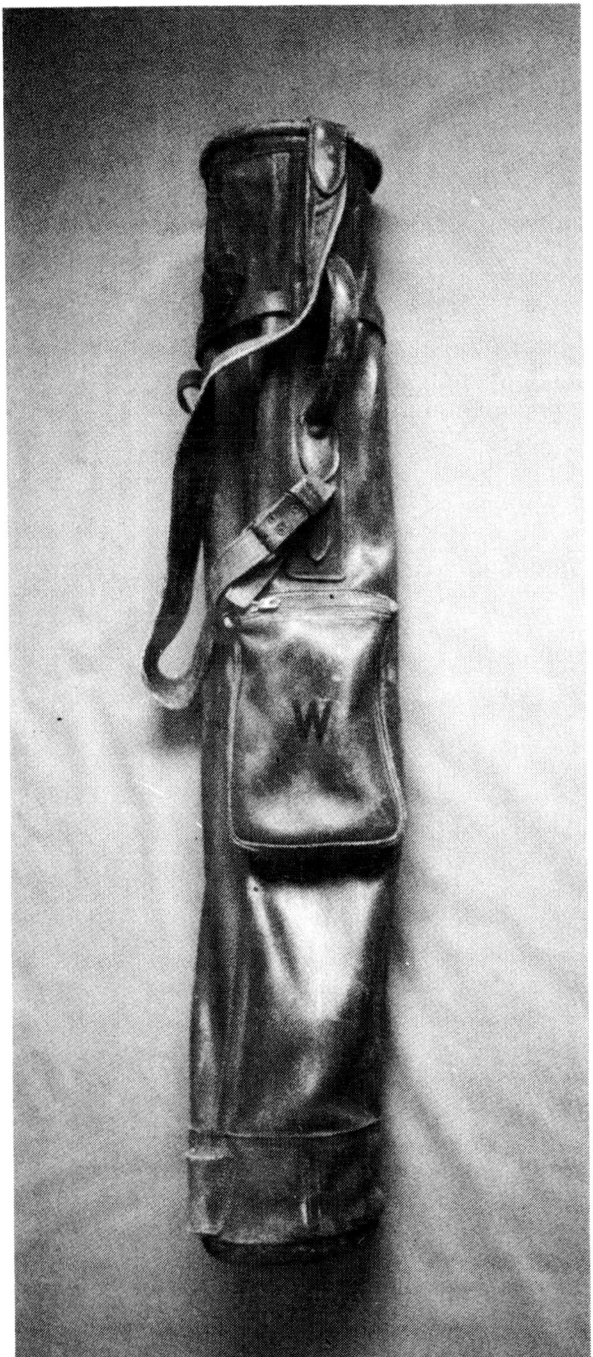

Left – The leather bag used by Willie Watt when he finished in joint seventh place in the 1923 Open Championship at Troon.

Dedicated to the memory of my Uncle James A. Watt
who taught me so much about golf.

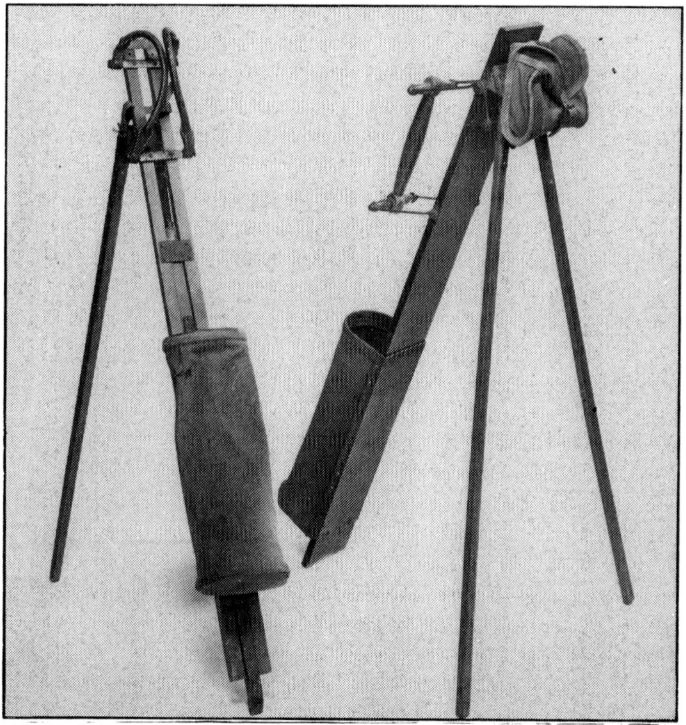

Early club carriers. L.-R. – An Osmond bag and a Bussey bag, both circa 1893.

INTRODUCTION

I CANNOT remember a time when I was not interested in golf.

Being born into a golfing family which, at that time, was proud to have five professionals amongst its members, talk of the game was a constant theme in my growing years. I loved nothing better than to listen to my grandfather, father and uncles on the subject; to the golfing personalities who visited North Berwick annually, for whom I would caddy at every opportunity as soon as I was old enough, became my heroes – as my autograph book still shows. One way or another, I absorbed a hotch potch of information on the game, most of it quite unconsciously.

It was a foregone conclusion that I would enter the golf trade, which I did by becoming apprenticed to my uncle James Watt, who was a renowned clubmaker, golf historian and a fine teacher. Those years with him and the ones that followed, when I, too, became a professional, provided practical experience which I am happily still finding a use for.

Although I left the trade in later years the game retained all its pleasure for me, and when my health dictated that I could no longer participate as a player, it was probably not surprising that I should turn to collecting as a way of continuing my involvement. I look upon it as a bonus that this aspect of the game has proved to be as fascinating and all-absorbing as any I have known.

This book represents a desire to share my enthusiasm with other collectors; to provide a glimpse into the origins and progress of the game up to the 1920s; and to assist the beginner in the recognition and identification of the old golfing clubs which go towards the building of a collection.

The text is mainly in two parts – the first covering the types of clubs used throughout various periods, and the second dealing with the craftsmen who turned their skills to the creation of the implements.

The professional who sold the woods generally had his name indented on the top of the club, whether he made the model or not. With the iron clubs, the blacksmiths usually stamped the reverse of the blade with a symbol or sign of their manufacture –

a mark which is now known as a cleek-mark. This is what the book is all about: a reference to the craftsmen and their wares.

There are, of course, some clubs and makers which we shall never be able to identify, but what has been researched has enabled me to write this small book, which will be a primer for those interested in the history of the Royal and Ancient game.

Over the years golf has given me great pleasure, both as a profession and a hobby, and I hope that by "putting pen to paper" I may have been able to give something back to the game. By collecting golf antiques we advance our knowledge of the game, help to unravel a little more of its history, and ensure the safekeeping of some of its artefacts – all of which I feel is very worthwhile.

A. A. W.

CONTENTS

1. HOW TO START COLLECTING

CALL it what you will, an interest, ambition, hobby or investment, the desire to possess a collection of golfing paraphernalia is now becoming a very fashionable pastime.

Considering golf is such an ancient game with its origins shrouded in the past, no implements or accoutrements of the sport which rooted itself in Scotland in the 14th/15th Century – and possibly before – have survived to give us any real idea of their original design and make up.

We are fortunate, however, that history has left us sufficient evidence of the game from the early 19th century and it is from this era that we will create our collection.

It is hoped that this small book will not only give guidance and encouragement to new collectors, but that readers who already own collections of which they are justly proud, will find items of interest which will add to their pleasure in this absorbing and fascinating hobby.

It is only in the past 15 years that individuals – save a handful involved with care of golf club-houses – have been smitten with the collecting bug, and during the last decade a Golf Collectors' Society has been formed with well over 1,500 enthusiastic members. Everyone is now becoming aware that old clubs, balls, books and other equipment have a unique history as well as a great value.

With novice collectors in mind and with the game of golf having such a very varied wealth of material still available, I would suggest that, without too great an outlay, an enthusiast could set the foundations by searching around for any clubs with a wooden shaft; items which were made from the turn of the century to approximately 1925. Such clubs, both wooden-headed and iron-headed may be purchased from around £3 apiece. There are also aluminium and brass headed clubs to be collected, they too have wooden shafts and are a little costlier. As manufacturing techniques improved and models and designs changed between 1870 and 1910, it is understandable that the prices will vary greatly and be reflected by the age of the club. (I will tell later of these changes prior to and during the early 1900's; they are quite complex).

However, this would be an initial framework and should collectors wish to raise their sights and try to obtain the true rarities of the Royal and Ancient game, they must anticipate high – sometimes inflated – prices which can and may only be acquired through the major auction houses.

Before becoming too absorbed in the ramifications of collecting, it is felt that a brief word on the early history of the game would be helpful.

As previously mentioned its origins *are* deep. It will always provoke argument and be ever controversial because sports played in the Low Countries with a ball and stick had a similarity to golf.

The Dutch, using crudely shaped hockey-like "clubs", played on frozen lakes and rivers, striking a wooden "ball" from one designated point to another. Also, around the hostelries, the game Kolven was played in a walled area – square or rectangular – the participants endeavouring to strike or get a ball as near to corner posts in the least number of shots. The discussions and disagreements are endless, suffice to say we British claim golf, in its present form, began in Scotland.

Whatever mode it took in the 14th and 15th centuries, the striking of a ball with a club, was fact.

Some historians suspect the game all began with seafarers returning across the North Sea from the Low Countries. On the journey they fashioned crude clubs and wooden balls with which they could play once they had come ashore. Frequently the seamen had long walks from port to their homes, so to break the monotony they "golfed" their way back, often playing from the dock-gates to their village inn or even the churchyard gates. Many lost both money and possessions by rash betting on the result of the game.

That this could happen is borne out by the fact that the land beside the firths and rivers on the East coast of Scotland in Fife and the Lothians sported the first "golf courses". It is also given credence by history providing evidence that the Stuart Kings and Mary Queen of Scots played in these localities.

In the 1450's to 1490's religious and regal displeasure of "the gowf" was apparent. Its interference with the necessity to practice archery and other defensive skills, led to a ban on it.

Thankfully in the early 1500's the game was alive again, being played by Royalty, the Courtiers, the Military and the more privileged sections of society, and by the middle of the century at least one lady golfer, Mary Queen of Scots, partook of the Royal and Ancient game.

Throughout the 1600's and 1700's progress was slow, though there is evidence of "by appointment" requests for clubs and balls from the Royal households of that period. The bow and arrow makers must have had to use all their skill and ingenuity to produce suitable requisites for the sport.

At this time, the first "courses" must have been fashioned. They were termed "links", the free areas where the local populace were at liberty to roam at will by the sea and adjacent land; usually very undulating and constantly being altered in places by the winds and tides which eroded flatter areas. The turf by the shore was kept short by rabbits and sheep, so green-keepers were an unknown breed. These were the ideal places to lay out "courses" and the earliest, of 5, 6 or 7 holes, are reputed to have been sited around Leith, Musselburgh, St. Andrews and other towns skirting the Firth of Forth

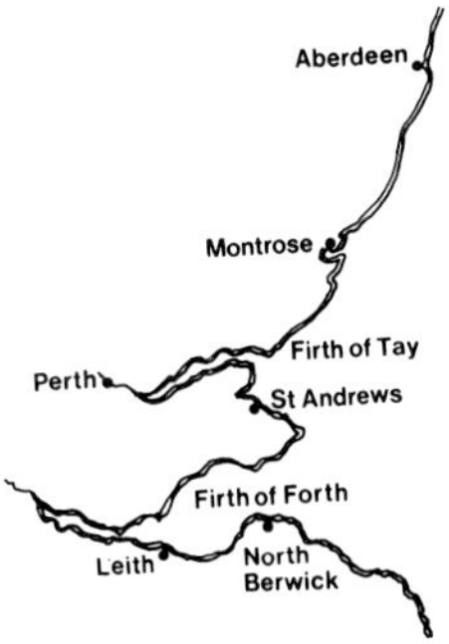

By the mid-1700's more people were participating in the game. It was a healthy outdoor leisure activity in which young and old could join. with improvements to the "play areas", to the wooden-headed golf clubs which became a little more refined, to the golf balls of leather (a round pouch crammed with feathers), the formation of Clubs, Societies and Associations occurred.

The game had also found its way to the United States of America.

In the late 1700's rough iron-headed clubs showed face. These were particularly made to move the ball from holes, scrapes and ruts, but unfortunately played havoc with the "feathery" golf ball. It is known that the early clubs were made by the skilled bow makers and carpenters attached to the Royal households, and from the early 1800's the makers of iron-headed clubs were called the cleek-makers.

Later, while I shall refer to one particular club as a "cleek", the same word will embrace a number of irons and putters.

Up to 1830 the game gathered momentum slowly, finally bursting into life around 1850. From then on – to the turn of the century – it swept on like a flood tide, mainly because it became within the reach of all classes. From this period of 1850 the golf societies and golf clubs which were in existence had laid out improved and extended golf links. They also employed "keepers of the green" (the equivalent of today's resident professional). To meet the large demand for the numerous clubs which were now being used, the shrewder craftsmen in the carpentry and blacksmith trades turned their hands to a new and novel industry.

The "professionals" who were responsible for the complete upkeep and running of the course had to purchase much of their stock from carpenters, certainly *all* of the iron-headed clubs from the blacksmiths, and were only able to turn out a few wooden-headed clubs themselves as they were fully occupied with everyday matters.

Understandably, the expansion brought into being more links and courses, more professionals and manufacturing companies and ball-makers to satisfy the players' needs.

This condensed history will, I trust, have given a nostalgic glimpse into the past and will prove beneficial when I come to describe items for the collection.

Should the appetite have been whetted and a few minds turned to the idea of creating a collection, one immediately wonders how to go about it. Initially a decision must be made as to its composition. Whether one concentrates upon putters only, whether it be the blacksmith's or cleek-maker's stamp on the iron-head, or whether it would be an assortment of many items.

To the absolute novice I would suggest the collecting of woods and irons only, the latter being of the "non-rustless" variety.

Firstly where to acquire such implements? At rural auctions, house-clearance sales, second-hand and junk shops, the now popular Sunday markets and jumble and car-boot sales; and of course your friends and neighbours who may have "treasures" in their garages, attics, cellars and out-houses. There are also a number of genuine dealers in golf memorabilia in the country where many of the clubs can be bought at very generous prices. Do not ignore the broken shafted club – the head may be quite rare – nor refuse anything just because the grip is missing, it would still be valuable. When it is identified by an experienced collector advice will be given regarding repair.

At this point I would like to emphasise that the names and stampings, particularly on irons, are not necessarily the makers of the clubs. They may well have been bought in unmarked, and finished off by the professional who stamped his own name thereon. Later this subject will be discussed in greater depth to enable one to recognise the pitfalls of buying fakes, "doctored" clubs and facsimilies which aspire to be antiques.

2. WOODS 1820-1920

IT TOOK a surprisingly long time for golfing equipment to attract the attention of those involved with antiques, but once interest was aroused it grew quickly and strongly, eventually becoming world-wide.

There is no close season for collecting, but without doubt the real treasures of the game start to come out of hibernation in the spring, when they are offered to connoisseurs and specialists through the major auction houses.

During the quest for clubs for a collection do not seek out only the relics and antiques, but look also for the old, the unique, the scarce and the many curious specimens which are to be found – curious sometimes for the illegality of their design; and sometimes for the way they represent the work of inventors and patentees who, no doubt with good faith and intention, were in danger of altering the sport, sometimes to the point of creating an altogether new game.

Understandably we would all like to own the most exclusive and desirable items available, but the very high prices they command, allied to their rarity, dictate that most of us start our collections in a modest way. Having said that, the category I will discuss in this chapter includes some of the most coveted, and therefore expensive, items still in existence.

Few clubs of the 18th century have survived, although fortunately Troon and St. Andrews own one or two very fine specimens, so we cannot reasonably expect to find anything of this period.

For practical purposes, therefore, I will concentrate on woods made between 1820 and 1920, although collections will mostly consist of clubs from 1840 on. This period was one of transition, notable for the modifications and variations in shape and size which took place – in many cases as a direct result of the alterations which were being made concurrently in the manufacture of golf balls.

We know that in this era the first sets comprised six to nine woods; old pictures depict how they were carried under the arm of the player or caddie, (the golf bag had not appeared in the mid 19th century).

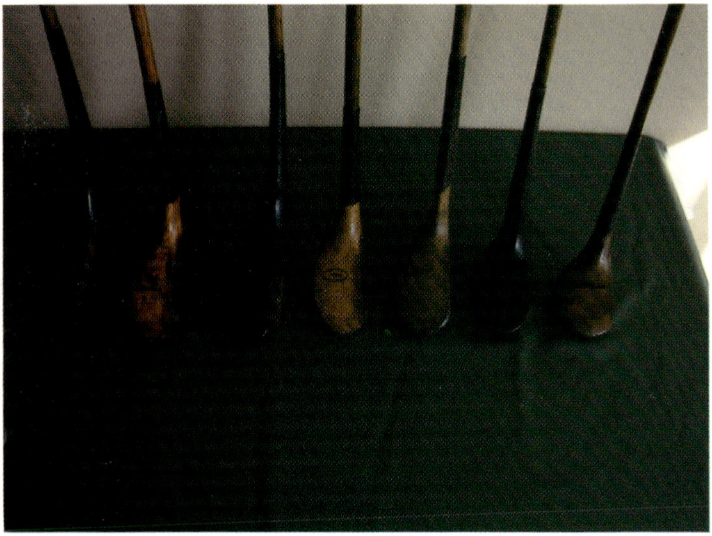

Early woods, from 1850 to 1900.

One might expect clubs of that comparatively early age to be crude, cumbersome and unwieldy, but this is far from the case. Depending upon the maker and the purpose for which the club was intended, heads were wonderfully elegant and streamlined, illustrating great craftsmanship and style. When fitted with a good shaft and grip, the balance and feel were such that they are still able to fire the collector with delight and admiration.

Sets were made up of:

1. *Play-clubs* (The Drivers)
   The plural is used here because two drivers were frequently carried as an insurance against a broken shaft. This long-headed club was used from the tee for distance, and was fitted with a long tapering shaft, being particularly slender just above the spliced joint. The grip was thickly padded to cushion mis-hit shots.
2. *Grassed Driver*
   Marginally shorter both in head and length, with slight loft on the face to lift the ball down-wind or off the better fairway lies. Many players omitted this club because it was much like the short spoon.
3. *Driving Putter*
   A stiff shafted wood for hitting the ball low into the wind, and for playing long running and approach shots over level ground to the green. The length of the shaft and head was similar to the Grassed Driver.

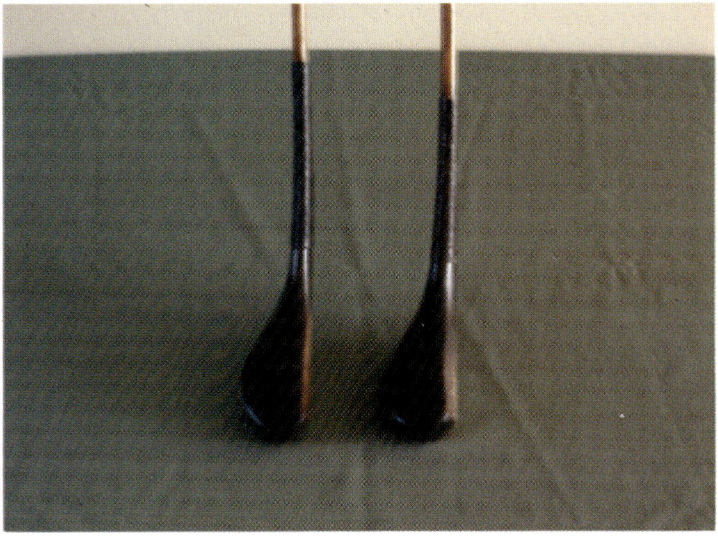

Driver, and Long-spoon of the mid 19th century.

McEwan dark stained driver and Forgan light keel stained driver.

4. *Long, Middle and Short Spoons*
   (Sometimes given the name of "scrapers"). For fairway lies and clearing hazards. They were much alike, differing only in length of shaft and with increasing degrees of loft.
5. *Baffing Spoon*
   "Baff" (on occasions "Biff" a Scottish word for strike or blow). In use the player would move plenty of turf with the

ball to create maximum lift and minimum run. Bearing in mind the ball was a "feathery", the run would not be great. The club had generous loft, was stiff in the shaft and the head was smaller.

6. *Wooden Niblick*
   Stiff shafted, well lofted, and well weighted to enable the ball to be moved from a bad lie whether in grass, sand or coarse rough.
7. *Wooden Putter*
   More upright in lie, surprisingly long in shaft and well weighted.

So how to recognise these implements?

Fig. 1 "Scared" or Spliced Wood

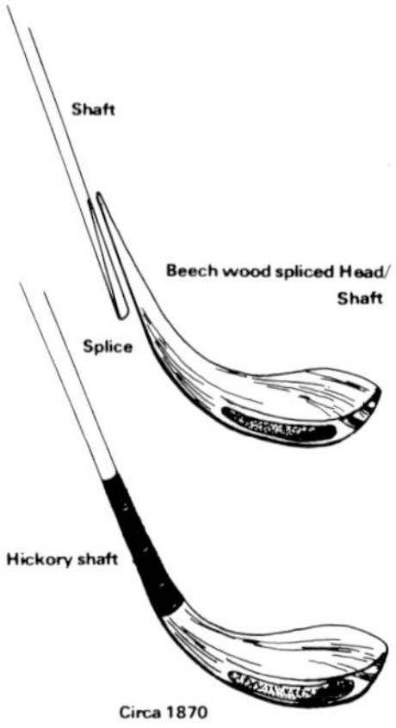

The collector will find that the term "spliced" or "scare-headed" ("scare" being a derivation of "scarf" – an overlapping joint) applies to all wooden clubs of this period. It describes how a long tapering shaft, cut at the thinner end with a splice of approximately some 4½″-6″ in length, fits a contra-splice on the socket of the clubhead (see Fig. 1).

The head, shapely and slender, of about 5″ long, 2″ wide and 1″-1½″ in depth, with the heel and neck of some 7″, tapered by the splice. A piece of ram's horn would be fitted in the leading edge of the sole – to minimise damage from stone, rock and flint, etc. – and the back of the head grooved to accept lead-weighting giving the club balance, feel and power.

The shaft was glued at its splice, then firmly bound with pitched twine to secure the two together; the shaft splice invariably showing at the neck of the club.

Of particular interest regarding the early longer woods is the flatness of the lie. This enabled the player to sweep at, instead of strike, the ball which, during the first-half of the 1800's, was the method of propelling it from tee to green.

In these early days when craftsmen had to use their ingenuity as well as their skill, much was done by trial and error to find the best materials to fashion the heads and the shafts. Hard woods had to be found which would withstand the onslaught delivered to the ball and terra firma, when beginners and the unskilled strove to obtain distance. Wood required "life" in it; resilience with solidity, and had to be as impervious as possible to splitting and cracking. In particular, it had to be well seasoned.

For the clubhead, beech was the most popular of all early woods, particularly the Scottish beech which, having been grown in cold exposed areas, was of a more robust quality. Other timber was tried; most of the fruit-woods – apple, pear and plum; the thornwoods; hornbeam, dogwood and holly; but clubmakers found so many inconsistencies in them, that they turned to American persimmon. This wood, therefore, provided a solution to the craftsmen's problem in the mid 1890's and it has survived to this day.

Having described the head, equal attention must be given to the shaft, so important to the balance of the club because of its length, strength, stiffness and position of "whip".

Ash was common in early times, also hazel: but lance-wood, greenheart and rose-wood were also given a trial, though I think the latter proved mainly suitable for putters. As with persimmon, the tough heavy hickory tree of the U.S.A. supplied fine straight-grained timber for the ideal shaft, and this was used from around 1860.

Hickory, a wood which was used for pickaxe handles, hammers and other tools, whilst being costly, proved the best alternative. Dependent upon the area in which the tree was grown and how the wood was sawn from the tree, enabled clubmakers to be selective, so for special clubs a white, red, natural or "ringed" variety could be fitted.

Hickory predominated until the arrival of the steel shaft a year or two after the First World War, and even after steel was legalised by the R. & A. in 1929, many golfers were reluctant to replace the clubs they had become so sentimentally attached to. I personally was replacing and fitting new wooden shafts – mainly into irons – throughout the latter half of the 1930's.

J. McEWAN
1st McEwan stamp

Having described the shape, composition and use of these clubs I have covered a period from about 1820 to 1870, and despite the arrival of two or three irons, most of them comprised the original sets. The play-clubs and spoons of the early era eventually became the driver, brassie, spoon and baffy, while the baffing spoon and niblick were the fore-runners of the lofting irons, mashie, mashie-niblick and niblicks of varying degrees of loft.

McEWAN

PHILP

COSSAR

CARRICK

JACKSON

MUNRO

Collectors who are fortunate enough to purchase or unearth these very early implements will find features of great interest and worth.

If the name is legible – usually in block letters on the head – and is stamped by one of the famous names such as McEwan, Philp, Cossar, Carrick, Jackson or Munro, each and all masters of their craft, these clubs will be costly, but what treasures; the first Chippendales of the golfing world!

Invariably the faces of the wooden clubs will be concave, and with the drivers there will be a distinct "toe-in" or hooked appearance, to avoid the torque of the club creating a cut or sliced stroke. The face may also have an insert of leather, bone, horn, ivory or composite rubber, which was either a prevention against, or a cure for, damage to a favourite club. Some players also believed the added facing gave extra length.

From 1850 to 1900 the improvements to the gutta percha ball – the successor to the feathery – became evident, as did the quality of the links and courses. It followed that the clubs would alter too, particularly the woods.

By the mid-1880's the long-headed model was being superseded by one with a head which was shorter and rounder. Firstly the "bulger" found a market. This was a near round head, with a convex face which, theoretically, should have reduced the degree of slice or hook if the ball was hit off the heel or toe of the club. It was successful, but the model looked unsightly, so many clubmakers with a mind and eye to selling something more attractive and functional, straightened the face and produced a pear-shaped streamlined design, which had much likeness to the present day woods. It became effective too.

At this time the various spoons were disappearing, though they too went through the alterations of design, mostly becoming smaller and compact, with the thick brass plates on the sole becoming thinner and in some cases covering only part of the base.

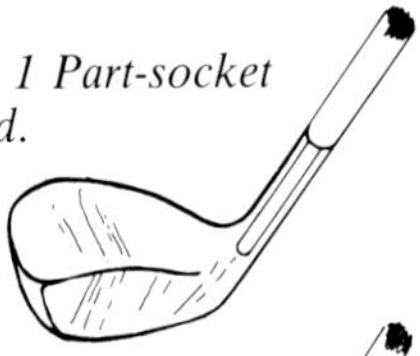
Fig. 1 Part-socket head.

Fig. 2 Through-socket head.

Around the late 1890's another important transition was taking place; the invention of the "socket head", a replacement to the splice. First models had a hole partly drilled down the thicker socket of the head; the shaft, without splice, was then inserted and well glued into the bore, finally being tightly bound with twine. Following shortly was the "through socket", the shaft going completely through to the sole, which is the fashion of most of the present day clubs (see Fig. 2). These latter wood socket implements are the clubs which the collector will find at the prices I mentioned earlier; the models of the first twenty years of this century.

Tangible and documentary evidence shows that the boom-time in golf really started in the 1860's, slowly at first, though gathering momentum. The first Open Championship took place in that year, so perhaps the reader will find it helpful if a further list of names of famous clubmakers is included. This is to assist the collector when deciding his or her purchase, it being relevant to the age and price of the club.

Following the McEwan, Philp era, we have the alliance of Philp/Forgan, so a club stamped with the joint names is a *real* collectors' piece. Others, such as Morris, Strath, Park, Dunn, Forgan (granted the Royal Warrant by the Prince of Wales in the mid 1860's), Forrester, Patrick, Hutchison, Wilson, Auchterlonie, Hunter, Beveridge, Sayers and Simpson all require a mention. They – not overlooking or forgetting their apprentices – were some of the founders of a great industry.

The names of craftsmen after the turn of the century such as Braid, Butchart (of "V" joint fame), Cawsey (socket and "scared" head clubs), Watt, Fernie, Hocking, Logan (specialist with holly), Martin, Riseborough, Ife, Sherlock, Turner (spliced and socket woods) and Whiting are, consequently, musts for the enthusiast to add to his collection.

So, hopefully, having convinced rather than confounded the would-be collector, and with the aid of the photographs and sketches, the information so far given can be summarised. Remember, I have concentrated on wooden-shafted "woods", a singular subject and the gateway to "getting into collecting".

PHILIP/FORGAN

TOM MORRIS

Tom Morris

W. PARK
MAKER
MUSSELBURGH

WM. PARK

STRATH

DUNN

R. FORGAN

HUTCHISON

1. The oldest and most expensive are the long-headed, shallow faced, spliced clubs. Flat in the lie; hopefully with a well-known maker's stamp of them; fitted with horn or face insert; dated 1840 onwards – very rare.
2. The shorter headed spliced club, bulged on face. Some without bulge, fitted with insert facings for gutta percha ball (after 1850). Baffing spoons a real scoop if found, particularly the long headed.
3. Smaller, narrow-headed woods (post 1870) with less hook, and with straight face. Seek Forgan woods with Prince of Wales feathers below the name stamp; later models becoming standardised, though still spliced. R. Forgan & Son woods from 1881.
4. Part socket and through socket clubs from early 1890's, with smaller attractive heads. Grips thinner to accommodate the hands using the overlap. Spliced clubs still about, used by the faithful, mostly the small baffy (now named wooden cleeks), useful for difficult lies and short rough.
5. Many woods of the 1900 to 1920 period are to be found; check shaft and clubhead in case they are cracked, look carefully for that little scourge, the wood-worm – don't take it into your collection if it is badly affected – keep a sharp look-out for modern clubs made to appear antique. Don't worry too much about the twine or "whipping" around the head or grip, it is

easily replaced. You will be able to learn of minor repairs and small renovations later. Contrary to opinion, there are many good "old-fashioned" club repairers about. They, too, are interested in collections and are ready to give advice, and help in restoration.

Long-nosed woods. Heads of beech, fruitwood and persimmon.

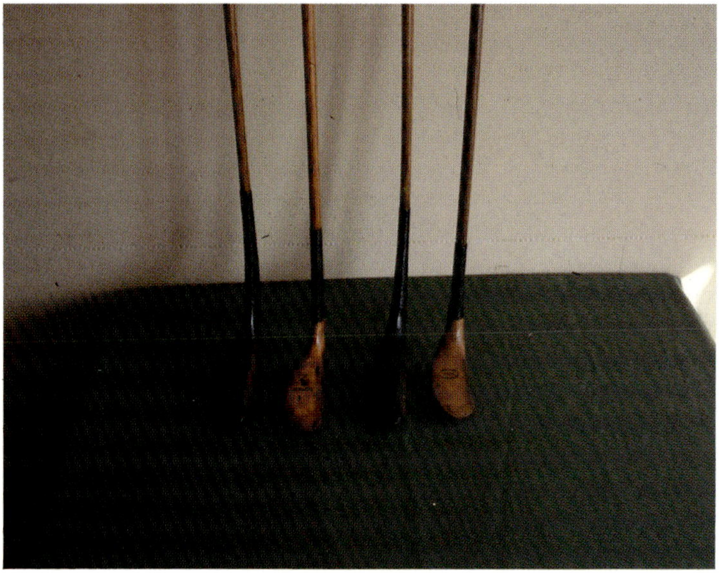

3. CLUB DEVELOPMENT

DURING the course of its history, the golf club has been fashioned in many diverse ways. It has been subjected to revolutionary modification and alteration, mostly in the head of the club, by shortening, weighting and restyling which, in modern idiom, is the ultimate in streamlining and tailoring.

Having concerned ourselves with the genesis and early development of wood clubs of the middle of the 19th century, we enter an era in which golf made immense strides in public favour. The game was being supported by players – old and young – who participated without ever hoping to arrive upon its roll of honour, but nevertheless dreamed their efforts would entitle them to be recognised as "golfers". It also brought the classes together; the artisan being able to play and score as ably as the upper-crust of society; and primarily it was a desirable and convenient avenue of exercise to those who wished to indulge in a non too energetic sport.

As season after season rolled on, more links and courses were designed and developed, and consequently more equipment and aids were required to fill the wants and needs of the addicted. How did the supply cope with the demand?

More clubmakers and instructors were needed, so while Societies, Associations and Clubs were being formed, the "keeper of the green", if he was employed by the club, (and who up to this time had been treated as a handy-man cum jack-of-all trades) found himself elevated to the exalted and respectable position of overseer, adviser and professional at the course.

These club professionals had to employ apprentices and assistants to make clubs, while at the same time small factories mushroomed to manufacture not only the woods, but the now popular iron clubs.

Digressing here for a moment, it may interest readers to know that, particularly in Scotland, in the early 20th century, the majority of professionals were freelance; they were not club-makers by trade, but were good instructors. (During the 1920's to late 1930's there were 8 professionals teaching at the North Berwick links; of course their work was seasonal).

With the upsurge in the game, particularly from the mid-

1880's, another breed of "clubmaker" appeared on the scene; he was the patentee, inventor and designer who, tinkering about with old, surplus and discarded clubs, introduced to the game a spate of hilarious, bizarre and often atrocious objects which no sane-minded player would ever test, far less purchase. Many contributors, however, did show ingenuity by producing serious items of interest, and while many were banned by the committee of the R. & A. they have re-appeared on today's scene.

However, back to the subject of collecting! Let us look first at the clubs I bypassed when you may recall, I listed those which were used by golfers as an addition or an alternative in their sets. Every one is a collector's piece, something to look for and acquire, if at a reasonable price.

I commence with a rarity.

Practical clubmaking at North Berwick.

1. *The One Piece Club*

The *true* one-piece club: a club of the second half of the 19th century, fashioned from ash, thornwood, dogwood or holly. The wood was taken from hedges and bushes grown on banks and steep slopes, so, using the root and the shoot as it grew, a natural curve was formed at the base.

The "one-piece" the collector is likely to find will be of ash. It has the root, with shoot or branch (upright) shaped into a complete club, from the toe of the head to the top of the "handle".

This club never was a favourite with apprentices or assistant clubmakers, the shaft really being in reverse of the normal style. Visualise the thick handle (grip) of a standard model, the shaft tapering thinly to the *head* of the club; then picture a shoot or branch growing from a root – thick at the base tapering to a point at the top. Great care had to be taken to shape and style the club, and it is little wonder there are not too many to be found.

A curious looking feature about it is the absence of whipping round the socket. It does make it a very desirable item to have in the collection, however, so again inspect everything carefully.

There is also a "relative" of the one-piece club; perhaps an idea which brought about W. Park's Compressed Patent. It is the same root with a socket of about 8″ but has a spliced hickory shaft in place of the original shoot.

The clubs are small headed, bulbous rather than long and are

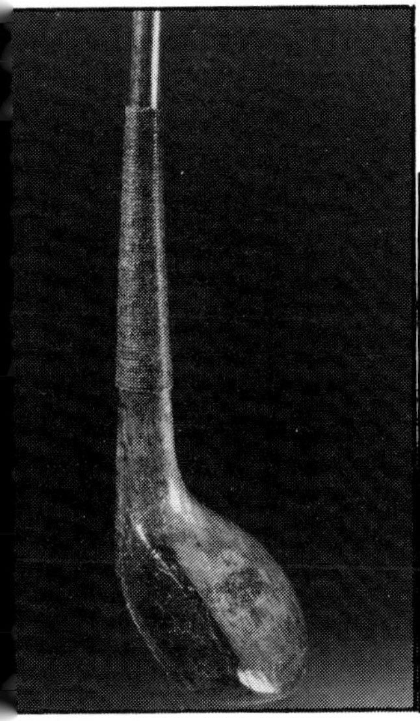

W. Park Jnr. Compressed Patent Driver.

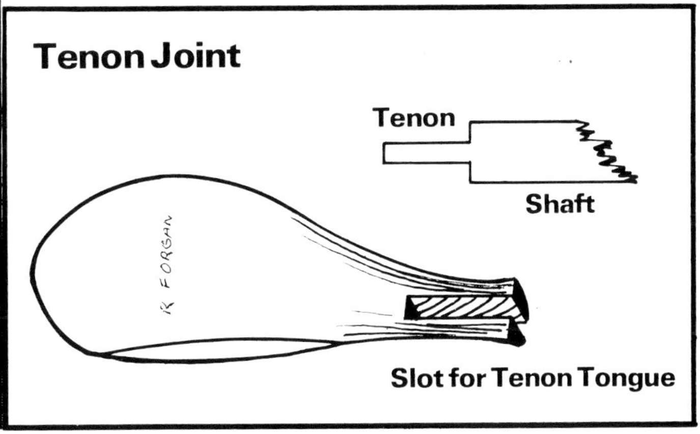

Tenon-joint head and shaft, by Forgan.

invariably light in colour.

Incidentally, perhaps better late than never, I suggest carrying a small magnifying glass (not a philatelist's glass) with you when you are looking closely at clubs, it will soon pay for itself!

2. *The Compressed Head*

A patent by W. Park in the 1890's. This was a flat piece of wood just under 2" thick, steamed and boiled until pliable; the wood was then bent until it formed the curve of the head and socket. The grain was consequently straight from the neck to the toe. Park's earliest heads were invariably finished with a yellow ochre "keel" (the clay-like substances mixed with water and linseed oil, used for dyeing, which were found mostly in the area of East Lothian between Aberlady and Dunbar).

The more collectable of the Compressed Patent is the left-handed wood – which usually had a face insert of thick leather or fibre. The number of these clubs made was small, as professionals encouraged right-handed play.

L/R. Approach Putter, Angle-shaft wood, Cane-shaft, The 'Dreadnought', The 'Bulldog'.

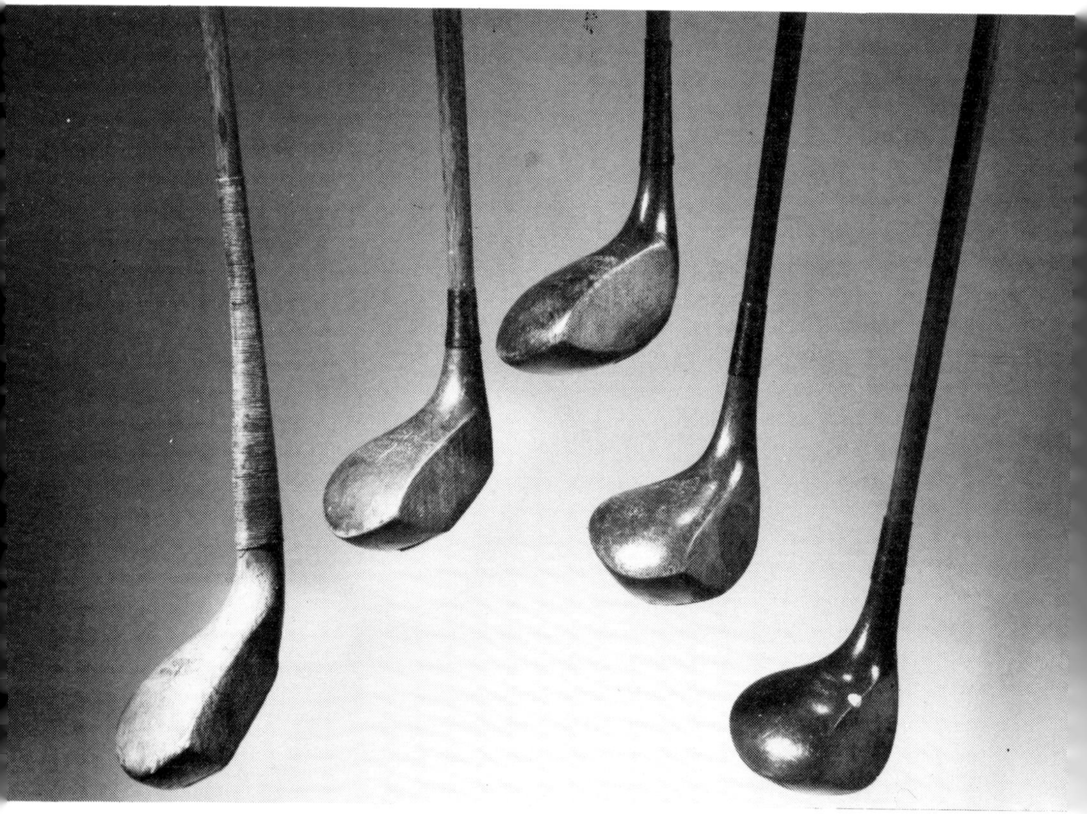

3. *Tenon Joint Clubs*

An alternative to the splice head. A tenon tongue was slotted into the wood socket and firmly bound after gluing. Only used by a few clubmakers as the whole was a lengthy and difficult process.

Collectors are advised to look closely at the neck of all wood-headed clubs in the hope that one may be a tenon joint. It will have a fairly long "binding".

4. *The Dreadnought*

A large round-headed socket club with a long, deep face. It is fairly flat on the base, also well weighted in order to give a springy kick in the shaft. Various woods were used in its manufacture. A number are stamped DREADNOUGHT, especially those made by Ben Sayers who made a claim to its invention. D. Anderson & Son of St. Andrews also produced a great variety even to the Junior Dreadnought, some with a half moon fibre face insert.

5. *The Bulldog*

A similar club to the above, though with a smaller head. The brassie and spoon are very rounded on the sole for removing the ball from "cuppy" lies. Many of these clubs, circa 1903, were fitted with rubber cloth grips. An intriguing specimen is that made by Forgan of St. Andrews; the head has no additions – no lead, no horn or plate on the sole and no facing insert, it was specially treated to keep the weight up to standard. It is a socket wood, some are stamped "Forganite".

6. *The "V" Joint Club*

Self explanatory really, patented by C. S. Butchart in the very early 1900's: a sturdy socket head with a "V" cut down towards the head to take a wedge pointed shaft. Well glued and bound at the joint.

7. *Angle-shaft Woods*

A "through socket-head" club fitted with a shaft which can only be described as anti-torque. A club produced about 1905/1910, which had the lower part of the shaft planed to an angle – right to left – causing it to be oval. Immediately under and below the grip, the shaft is round. I have seen and possess only drivers and brassies of this style. The brassie will probably have the plate wholly covering the sole. R. Forgan & Son turned out a considerable quantity.

8. *Cane Shafted Woods*

Although these clubs are post 1920, I mention them as they are complementary to a collection; a novel idea from the "House" of

Hardy Bros. Alnwick, England, known throughout the world for the excellence of the fishing rods they manufacture.

The shaft is made up of 12 pieces of wedge-shaped bamboo. Six thin parts were glued together to form a slender shaft, this was then covered by a further 6 pieces, making a strong six-sided shaft. A considerable number of sets were sold, but inclement weather took its toll, the damage being caused by the torque (twist) of the head splitting the shaft. Jack White (Open Champion of 1904) was the most enthusiastic professional to use them and many to be found today have his name on them. He sadly saw them fade away, steel shafts being the "in" thing by the late 1920's. At least one cane shafted club, however, is worth having in the collection. Incidentally if the club is an iron head, it will probably be rustless. Most shafts are stamped PALAKONA, along with the manufacturer's name and address.

Having looked at the wood-headed clubs, all very usable even if some were short lived, I now approach the most important and probably the most abused and maligned club in the player's set.

The Putter

As that fine amateur, Roger Wethered, once said, "the game would be nothing without the troublesome business round the hole; the green and the putter delivers the final verdict, an act of relentless golfing justice is done".

Whereas the old woods of by-gone days will possess an interest as a museum piece, an aged putter instils a feeling of reverence and, in most cases, a faith that the owner bestows on a valued and trusty retainer. Having previously described the Driving Putter, many golfers also carried an *Approach Putter*, a wooden club with a short, stiff shaft and with loft for playing over patchy ground to the green, used mainly on the flatter links such as St. Andrews and Musselburgh. It was affectionately known as the "Musselburgh iron". The club is recognisable by its loft and length.

The Putter (for the green)

The "green" in the early to mid 1800's was an extremely small area, some 15 feet across; it was also the teeing ground to the following hole. The ball which could be teed on sand to a height of 8″ had to be driven from within 8 feet of the flagstick. The surface of the green was not smoothly trimmed, it being rough and uneven due to constant stamping of foot by beast and man, so putting became something of a lottery. The players who "holed out" with regularity became the "great putters" of their day.

Putters of the pre-gutta days were invariably long-headed – slightly shorter and more upright than the play clubs. From early times Hugh Philp – who was recognised as a master craftsman of wood putters – usually fashioned his heads a little broader than his contemporaries; they command a premium, so if you acquire one, you will be the envy of your friends.

Putters were surprisingly heavy and one surmises this was created to counteract the vagaries of the ball and the green. Following the introduction of the gutta ball, professionals and clubmakers at seaside links made and used a shallow-faced putter in the summer for hard fast greens and a deeper faced club for winter use on slow greens and bumpy surfaces. (Does this idea still not give food for thought?)

Later in the 19th century putter heads became shorter; with a straight face, a graceful bow to the back and a neck curved with symmetry, to the shaft. The sole or base – fitted with horn – had a width suitable for the club "sitting" rather than being manoeuvred into position on the turf.

As the feathery had long left the scene, and the "gutty" improved, so did the putters. It is a well-known and indisputable axiom that numerous clubmakers who were good players, produced putters of superb quality and workmanship, so these clubs were receiving more attention than any other.

It is interesting to see the similarity of design in the early McEwan putter, and that of Park; they are beautifully stream-

Left – Long-nosed beech headed putter and Vulcanite putter.

Below – A 'special' used in 1895, a centre – Shafted putter, a socket putter, and a spliced putter.

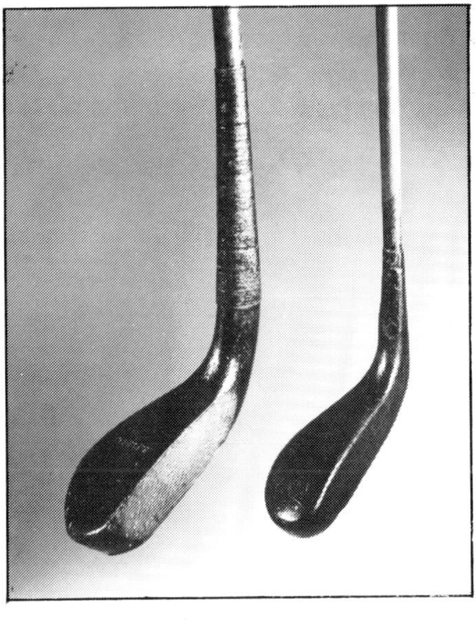

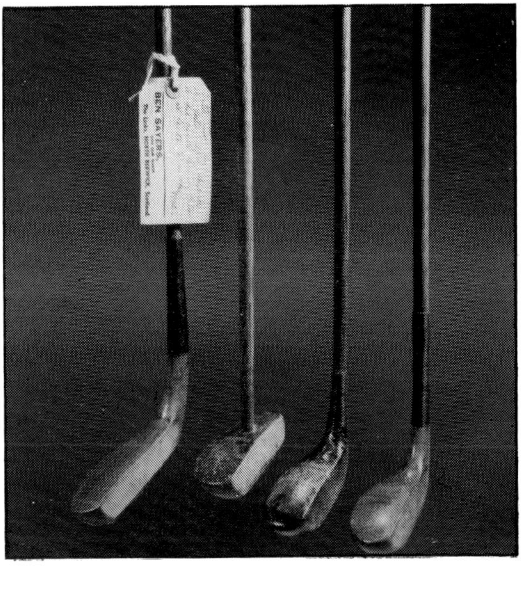

lined, pear-shaped at the back with fairly upright curved sockets. Clubs that feel "good" in the hands.

Towards the end of the century "part socket" and "through socket" putters were popular, mainly because of the shorter head and neck, with a distinctly upright lie, giving a fine balance; the first wooden putters which could be used with a pendulum motion.

An innovation to the putter was a deliberate curving or bowing of the shaft, which would place the hands in a line behind the clubhead: this necessitated a lightening of the clubhead – some of the lead weight being removed – to retain the balance and "feel" of the putter. The idea did not last too long, however, as iron putting cleeks had found favour by this time.

For the collector, a putter worth looking for is the "square-headed" two and three faced club. Patented by J. Brown in the 1890's, it could be used in two or three ways, croquet style, using the toe, secondly right-handed and lastly three-faced if left-handed. (J. Gassiat made a similar club.)

A putter with a rectangular head and centre shaft is also to be found. It was short in the shaft and was well balanced. It was in use for some time before the R. & A. eventually banned it in 1909. (It returned, however, in the 1950's.) J. Carruthers designed a wooden putter with an extremely concave face, his theory probably being that if the ball was struck off-centre, the heel or toe would counteract a misdirected line.

Wooden putters not being part of a "set" of clubs, kept their design for many years, varying only in the shape of the head. Even while iron putters and putting cleeks were in vogue, the wooden-head was still being manufactured and sold, and who knows their return to fashion may not be long delayed.

Aluminium Heads (wooden shafted)

First knowledge of this material used in clubs was about 1896, and they really went into production about 1902. There were 3 or 4 manufacturers, but the most prolific was Mills of Sunderland. That company made all clubs from driver to cleek, niblick and putter, the latter being turned out in their thousands – I have possessed over 36 different models, and I am certain many others are about. The company "split up", becoming The Standard Golf Co. and The Imperial Golf Co. The Sunderland Golf Co. Mills name was retained and produced putters for all the famous players of the early 1900's – Braid, Ray, Duncan, etc. so look for the "Autographed". Special features about the clubs were the detail given on the sole – incidentally they are mostly socket clubs. Drivers, spoons and cleeks were numbered 1, 1½, 2, 2½, 3 and so on, the cleek was also stamped and numbered, as were mashies and niblicks.

Some putters had a veritable history upon the sole. It could have the maker's stamp (i.e. Braid-Mills), and reference number: the lie of the club – "upright lie", "medium lie" or "flat lie", the weight of the club, 9 oz. 5 dms or 10 oz. 2 dms. I suppose it was the "personalised" club of its day. Collectors who wish to specialise in one particular aspect of golfing equipment can have great fun amassing the various aluminium putters; all have slight variations in or on the head, and the "oldies" to look for are the long-headed clubs; also those with the deliberate bow in the shaft. Probably one of the most famous of the aluminium range is a copy of the Schenectady club: a near centre-shafted putter patented by A. F. Knight of Schenectady, New York, in 1903, and used by W. J. Travis to win the British Amateur Championship in 1904; it is a must for a collection.

Brass too was fashionable for putters. The first being straight bladed clubs, which could be used right or left handed. Later models followed the style of the wooden putters, though with smaller heads.

In addition to the putters already described, the collector will be able to find others fashioned from materials of various composition. Buy for your collection the old design in vulcanite, ebonite – a nice long-headed putter – moulded gutta percha and laminated leather (perpendicular strips glued and hardened), able to be worked on as wood.

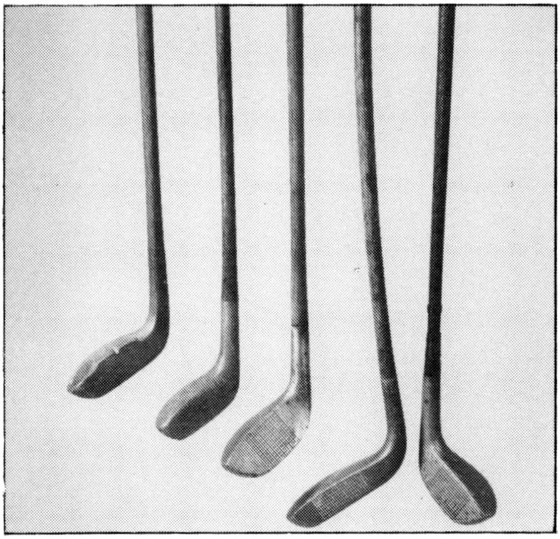

Assorted aluminium clubs

Having given the essential wood heads and shafts an introduction, just a word or two about "the other end" – the "handle" or "grip".

The oldest clubs have the thickest grips, for wrapping both hands around, just as with a cricket bat. These were made usually of calf-skin, sheepskin, cowhide and "shammy" (from goat or chamois). According to the desire of the clubmaker, the grip could be bound on with either surface outward; the smooth treated side eventually becoming the more popular. From the mid-19th century the grip with padding was very thick; by the end of the 1800's it was considerably thinner and nicely tapered.

As I mentioned earlier, golf was the sport of the masses by 1885 and so along with the craftsmen who were busily making the game easier, came the eccentrics with their ideas and inventions all hoping to find fame and fortune. Both woods and irons became ghosts of golf clubs, and are too numerous to relate; but for interest I will try to describe one or two of the early woods.

Drivers in the 1890's with a complete face insert of thick hippopotamus; rhinoceros; bull-seal or elephant hide for striking the ball.

1898 – a wooden head fitted with a pneumatic cushion which could be inflated from the back of the club. Heavy brass plate on the sole.

1901 – a clubhead with a brace connecting the head and the shaft angled from the top of the splice to the toe of the club.

1904 – a spring inserted behind the face of the club, then wound up by a key creating a tension until the ball was struck.

1907 – driver with two aluminium rollers inserted into sole (a well made and nicely balanced club this, but what an incredible sound when the ball was hit)!

Circa 1910. In the Lothians, a clubmaker was instructed to make a driver, without lead – drill a ¾″ hole in the back of the club to within ¼″ of the face; partly fill with mercury, then plug hole. The result? Shots O.K. for about a week or two, then when the clubface was damp, it caved in. It was never patented – it was too comical to contemplate.

Many other humorous oddities were created, the majority having springs, rollers, ball bearings and heavy liquids to give push and power to striking the ball. Most were illegal. There is also a fabulous cane shafted "fishing rod" driver to be acquired for a collection. The "whip" is so great that anyone trying it should watch out for a whack on the left knee-cap from the clubhead should the backswing be too fast.

4. THE FIRST GENERATION OF IRON CLUBS

FORTUNATELY no game has a richer array of tools and accoutrements than golf, nor has commercial rivalry, in itself, found so much scope to contribute such wealth through design and development to make a game easier if not more enjoyable.

Having some 500 years behind it, time has been on our side to make this expansion, but in fact the production and manufacture of the clubs we possess lie within the confines of the past two centuries.

I have described many of the wooden clubs of the early 19th and 20th centuries previously and now give the arena to the iron clubs, the implements which in some ways were, and are, tantamount to being the weapons of the gladiators.

Golf in *early* times was a difficult game, players had to "manufacture" shots and manoeuvre the ball from hole to hole with only a handful of clubs, but by the 1920's there were sufficient clubs designed to play every conceivable shot. There is no doubt that the irons helped to alter the game, and in their evolution replaced a serene and relaxing activity with something

An early putting cleek by Carrick, circa 1865.

CARRICK

CARRICK

BISHOP & HENDRY
LEITH

R. CONDIE
ST. ANDREWS

W. GIBSON & CO. LTD.
KINGHORN

Harrower
Carnoustie

more akin to a labour abundant with mechanics and science.

I described the materials and make-up of the wooden-headed clubs and will do so with the iron clubs, but the subject is a much greater and more complex one, so it requires breaking down and dividing into varying eras and categories.

A clarification may help at this juncture. Hundreds of clubmakers could turn out *wooden-headed* clubs and it was not only the professionals, but joiners, cabinet-makers and other handymen able to use a saw, rasp, file, chisel and sandpaper who fashioned them, even for their own use. With the *iron-headed* club, only blacksmiths, iron-smiths and the man with an anvil and forge could produce such a head, consequently in the earliest days they were not only difficult to obtain, but were crude and unwieldy in style.

As the subject is one of immense variety and interest and so many different irons have been produced to fulfil so many functions, it will help readers who wish to select them for their collection if they are put into periods of manufacture; giving me the opportunity of describing not only the model and design of the club, but naming some of the makers. I also think this is an appropriate time to bring up the subject of the blacksmith's stamp – alias cleekmark – on the majority of iron heads.

In the days of Philp, Wilson, McEwan, etc., only the name was stamped on the club blade. Carrick alone from a similar period deciding to identify his work with the mark of a cross or crosses. From the 1870's other makers' symbols arrived though some, for example Park, Jackson and Dunn, persisted with their name only. But the motif idea was catching on, and by the latter quarter of the 1800's dozens of professionals and manufacturers had one or more stamp marks on the reverse side of their iron heads.

This mark enables the collector to identify where the club originated and will, to a great extent, date it. As a guide, the beginner will find the Anvil or Hammer design of Spalding; a Bishop's Mitre (Hendry & Bishop); a Rose (Condie); a Star (Gibson); a Clay Pipe (Stewart); and a Heart (Harrower) popular discoveries, but there are over 100 different cleekmarks (not necessarily 100 different makers).

So gather as many different cleekmarks as possible, the collection will grow to something worthwhile.

From the early 19th century to the first quarter of the 20th century, there were what might be loosely termed four generations of iron club.

The cleek was the first of the long irons.

A few irons of the 1700's exist, but they, while being treasured by their owners, are rough and pitted with age, so it is nigh impossible to put anything like an accurate date of manufacture on them. They are unstamped and nameless, but their weight, the shape of the head – dented by hammering – and the thick lengthy sockets and extremely strong shafts fitted with well padded grips, give clues to the generation to which they belong.

Having stated the earlier clubs are of the later 1700's, I must mention Mr Steven Van Hengel, authoritative Dutch author of *Early Golf*, who quotes "of Kolfers, one of them putting while kneeling, using the club the construction of the head likely to be iron rather than lead".

This was taking place in Holland in the 16th century – but was it golf as played in our own Isles? I think not!

In Britain, I feel sure other 18th century iron relics *do* exist – probably without shafts – and are still hiding themselves away in the most unlikely places; particularly in or near the sites of links or courses which no longer exist; let us hope that someday someone may unearth them; it is our greatest wish to find something more ancient than those at present on display.

Keeping things in perspective, and before describing the types of irons that are most collectable, permit me to put all of them in their categories, according to their era. In other words a blanket coverage from 1775 onwards.

The track iron – "rut iron" – in my view has true status in golf. It was the harbinger of good tidings to players unable to extricate the ball from the "impossible" lies, and because of the particular and singular difficulties of the links it is manifestly clear that with its arrival no golfer could afford to be without it.

The lofter, the cleek, the sand iron and putting cleeks gradually formed a union with, or ousted, the shorter and lofted wooden clubs and this concluded the "first generation".

In the "second generation" of clubs, circa 1870, we had the arrival of the driving and lofting cleek – with varying depth of face – the rut niblick and mashie, also the straight-bladed putter.

Following on their heels came the anti-shank models, the driving iron, driving mashie and the wryneck putter. Blacksmiths' stamps also appeared.

The "third generation", around the turn of the 20th century, heralded the birth of the mid-iron, push-iron, jigger, sammy, pitcher, chipper, sand and water irons; mashie-irons with varying blades, such as "deep-faced", "long-faced", spade and even midget mashie (a full-sized club), the mashie niblick and niblick and of course by this time aluminium clubs were in use.

Finally, my "fourth generation", up to the mid 1920's. The irons were being given model names, as well as stamps. Some of the better known for the collector to watch out for are – Maxwell, Genii, Ace, Cardinal, Accurate, Orion, Triumph, Confidus, the Benny and many others; in fact there is fun and interest in collecting named models in their own right, they are so numerous.

Following the naming of clubs, came the numberings: half-sets and full sets were being made up, and these had anything from No. 2 to No. 8 stamped on the back of the club or the sole. (If a No. 1 was required for the set, it would be specially made. The straightness of the face made it the least popular club.)

So now you have a rough idea of the periods of manufacture; I have also given a few names which have covered a wide span.

Before going into deeper detail about the type and use of the various clubs, let me clarify a matter which causes much confusion throughout collecting.

Whatever name is stamped on a club, it is often accepted as the maker's work. This is *not* necessarily the case, particularly with the club professional.

Let us imagine the professional at a golf club getting low on stock! He urgently requires 12 assorted woods; these he would order from a manufacturer and receive them unstamped (sometimes ungripped and occasionally unpolished). Upon receipt he would stamp his own name on the clubs, "grip" them and finish them off ready for display or sale. He also required irons! He *could* order the finished clubs (already stamped with his name); or he would separately order the heads (stamped); shafts and grips, etc., then assemble the clubs or sets to whatever specification he desired. Much of the work of these professionals from about 1900 was assembly not manufacture, certainly with the irons.

This meant many of the major companies held name-stamps for hundreds of professionals.

Throughout the 170 years I have been covering – 1750/1920 – I have briefly categorised the clubs of their times. This only affects the period from their introduction, many modifications and adjustments being tried and tested during a club's lifetime.

To the newcomer pursuing the building of a collection I emphasise that when iron heads were being mass produced, the characteristics, sizes and shapes of particular models did not match or conform. In many cases while the back of a club matched another, the faces could differ, one having punch marks, while the other was lined or scored. This particularly applied to drop forged heads – from the turn of the century – when it was discovered that a "rough" surface gave grip to the ball. Prior to 1900 most irons were smooth faced.

JN. GRAY

The *very* early iron makers – cleekmakers – such as Carrick, White, Gray, Wilson, etc., made the majority of their own irons; though rough and unstamped in many instances some are identifiable by the shape of the heads.

Jn. GRAY
PRESTWICK

By the middle of the 19th century clubmakers such as Dunn, Strath, McEwan, Jackson and Park were having heads forged by local blacksmiths; Park having at least three local smiths hand-forging heads for him in their own workshops.

By 1890 small and large factories were hammering out countless numbers of irons of many shapes and sizes and with the quality of the ball improving, together with the reliability of the shaft, clubs had a longer life. Common to jungle law, manufacture gradually became "the survival of the fittest", so the number of cleekmakers became less and less. A plaintive cry

from a clubmaker in a copy of *Golf Monthly* of 1912 highlights the situation of that year. He states "The number of manufacturers making iron heads in Scotland is now down to about a dozen; one is in the hands of the receiver and another has decided to shut up shop and retire." For this to happen was tragic to many, but as the larger companies continued and the game expanded – worldwide – the good man manufacturers' names became synonymous with golf.

Scotland, as I have claimed, created the game; with resident suppliers of golfing equipment providing such famous names as Stewart, Forgan, Gibson, Nicoll, Condie, Cochrane, Gourlay, Anderson of St. Andrews (one of the largest iron-head makers), Anderson of Anstruther, Hendry & Bishop, Harrower and Winton. In England, Ayres, A.N.C.S.L., Halley, Spalding, Benetfink and Slazenger. These companies were the backbone of the trade where irons were concerned and it is interesting to find they frequently made heads for one another; this being proven by having two different stamps or cleekmarks on the club. Collectors are advised to look for the irons with more than one cleekmark.

You have now been given the names and types of iron-headed clubs which were used during specific periods, along with some names of the makers and manufacturers. From now on, starting with the earliest irons which are the rarer and more expensive, I

Track irons (with a feathery and a gutty ball).

will describe the desirable items to look for, while at the same time detailing their function.

To the best of our knowledge the intrusion of the iron-head came about in the second-half of the 18th century, the first of these implements being the *Track Iron*. This club, just under three feet in length, was probably the heaviest in the bag. It had the thickest, longest hosel – or socket – deeply and unevenly nicked by cold chisel at the end; a strong, seasoned ash, hazel or greenheart shaft and bulky grip, and had a very thick small head, little larger than the golf ball itself – which before 1850 was "feathery". Being hand-hammered it would have no face markings and was probably unnamed. The purpose of this club, as it name suggests, was to remove the ball from cart tracks and horse hoof-prints where they had crossed the links to collect sand from the shore. The other problem, "sheep shelters" – rough hollows and banks hewn out by animals seeking cover from the elements – which were the precursor of the bunker, gave the "rutter" a rightful place alongside the wooden niblick. While seeking the track iron, it is probable a short-socketed model will turn up, it too is for the collector as the characteristics and functions are the same; a club of uncertain birth.

With the track-irons safely established in the early sets, other models were now being fashioned.

The Lofter – or lofting iron, was probably second in line. This

Sand iron and lofter

club became the successor of the Short Spoon and Baffing Spoon, it being endowed with a deep curved blade some 4½″ long, thicker at the base and with generous loft. The socket was akin to the track iron, long and thick to support a strong shaft.

In the footsteps of that club came –

The Cleek. I often ponder how this club got its name: cleek (cleak) is an old Scottish word given to the tool or implement used by someone cutting weeds, grass or corn with a hand sickle: it is a stick with a short reverse fork at one end to hold the grass in position while it is cut. I see no connection between the two instruments.

To return to the cleek, which was the first of the "driving" irons. The blade was similar in length to that of the lofter, shallower in the face and with less loft. The socket was less bulky, as was the shaft, and the club played the part of a long to mid-spoon.

There are various designs of cleek heads to be found; some of the first were made with parallel blades, many had slight depth at the toe narrowing to the socket. The loft varied marginally too, this being dependent upon the manufacturer.

I remind the reader at this stage that I have covered the period up to the middle of the 19th century. The game had changed in as much as iron clubs *had* arrived; golf courses and links were being properly formed – whatever number of holes they had – golf balls had improved, particularly in 1848 when the gutta percha ball was invented and the feathery was being replaced. Fashion, they say, dies hard, however, so it is more than likely that the gutta ball, smooth and round, veering and dipping as it flew, took a couple of years to come into its own, and players also took time to become accustomed to a new sound of club against ball. The method of propelling the ball had changed too. From sweeping, flat swings, activating maximum run, the swing was grooved in a more upright fashion, giving carry and lift to the ball, which called for less improvisation on the part of the player.

The Iron-headed putting cleek. This implement, with slight loft, became a rival of the wooden-headed putter; it served a variety of purposes as it could be used off the green as well as on. Many players just altered the position of their stance to deal with the shot being played. It was ideal for bumpy greens.

Having described the implements of the pioneers, a mention is necessary at this stage regarding faked, "doctored" and refurbished clubs, many of which have been sold to the unseasoned collector as genuine articles.

Many replicas are being manufactured, particularly wooden-headed clubs of every model – driver to putter. When these are sold openly as copies, they serve a purpose; the danger arises when they are deliberately offered as an antique. I have seen a considerable number which have been so cleverly camouflaged that only close scrutiny gave the game away.

Later I shall give further mention to the unscrupulous interference of clubs, but whenever you see a well polished club, with new horn and new grip, treat it with caution. Also watch out for the black/white pitched twine.

With the irons, the track-iron is fair game for trickery. Soon after the track iron, came the rut niblick, and in many instances the two cause confusion, even at auctions. The old rut niblick with a head of similar thickness to the track-iron can easily have the head reduced to a small size, and with a bit of knocking about and rough treatment, the heads are fashioned to look similar.

Never be tempted to buff or highly polish an antique iron. Few clubs require restoration and renovation to a degree which will make them look converted rather than restored. Antiques worth keeping must be recognisable as such, so please treat them lightly and delicately, otherwise find someone in the trade, preferably an older clubmaker who will not fit the hickory shafts in back-to-front, or use polyurathane varnish over the lead in a wooden clubhead. Leave repairs to someone with experience.

Should readers wonder why I have briefly mentioned fakes, etc. at this stage, I did so deliberately, knowing that the *very old* and venerable clubs about which I have been writing – the track-iron, the lofter, the cleeks (driving and putting) and the sand-iron are particularly prone to faking, causing doubt and concern to the collector. The unscrupulous will soon foist them upon the unwary.

5. THE SECOND GENERATION OF CLUBS

I CANNOT do better than begin this chapter by quoting words taken from an advertisement I came across while browsing through an old 1903 catalogue which I received from a well-known St. Andrews clubmaker. They are delightfully indicative of their day, confirming the Royal and Ancient game *was* originally one of leisure and pleasure.

The advertisement reads:

"These clubs which we invented *many years ago* are old favourites, and they are in greater demand than ever, proving that they have made many friends."

This reference coincides with my "second generation" of clubs; and introduces further cleeks, putters, niblicks and mashies, etc. which, in effect, extended the assortment of wood and metal clubs being used in the sport.

Before dealing with the clubs however, let me mention the progress of the game. During the middle of the 19th century when the "keeper of the green" became the appointed professional to a golf club, many of these gentlemen were becoming skilful golfers, bringing into the game the competitive spirit which understandably created rivalry; friendly but nevertheless serious.

Challenge matches as well as private matches were becoming popular, particularly when a wealthy "backer" – or consortium of "backers" – could be found to promote a "battle royal". Many matches, in fact, were played with hundreds of pounds at stake, and huge crowds came from surprising distances to give support to their favourites.

Some of these games were taking place before 1858, the year of the first inter-club major tournament, which was promoted by the Prestwick Club, designed for teams of amateurs. Teams from a dozen major clubs were invited to St. Andrews to play in a "knock-out" tournament for a Silver Cup. The "championship" (as it was titled) was so successful that it was repeated in 1859 and 1860. With the amateurs now stealing the headlines it was decided a Championship for professionals be inaugurated and, in October, 1860 the first professional "Open" took place. (The following year amateurs were permitted to enter!). The Prestwick Club again hosted the Championship, and as the sum of five guineas was all that a "collection" produced, a broad Red Leather Belt adorned with Silver Plates was purchased by the club as a trophy, which was worth considerably more to the winner – prestige wise.

Playing on the Prestwick links, 3 rounds of 12 holes each, Willie Park Senior, professional at Musselburgh links, became the first winner, he being one of the eight players entered. He took the title of Open Champion with a score of 174, an average of 58 per round.

Prestwick was the venue for the first 11 years playing for the Belt, and it was presented to young Tom Morris after his three successive wins in 1868, '69 and '70. In 1871 the Championship did not take place, but was resurrected and won again by Morris Junior in 1872; the trophy, however, was now a Championship Cup (for amateurs and professionals). In 1873 the venue was changed and St. Andrews proudly housed its first Open Championship.

The stories of the early Championships with the colourful and delightful characters who took part in them, make wonderful reading. When one considers the types and conditions of the links; (the Open was and is always played on a seaside links – I hope it will never be otherwise!) the make up of the clubs, the balls, and the rules which deemed "the ball be played from where

At Ganton. W. Park Jnr., driving in the great match against H. Vardon in 1899.

it lies", one can readily equate the prowess of these players with the "greats" of today. What, might one ask, would the eight participants of the 1860 Open Championship have thought of the present day Championship? Perhaps they look down smiling at the "frenzy" of it all.

By this time many of you are asking what this information has to do with "collecting"! It is included for the benefit of those golfers, young and old, who know little of the game's history and its relationship to golf clubs. I have used the Open Championship as the spring-board for further description of the clubs of that era.

Before and throughout the 1870's the sets were comprised of a mixture of wooden-headed and iron-headed clubs. However, like "progress, which never stands still", the revolution in the manufacturing of clubs, whether by hand or machine, gathered momentum, and by 1890 thousands of implements were being made, and dozens of courses being laid. I hazard a guess that during the next 15/20 years literally hundreds of golf clubs will celebrate their centenary year.

Reverting to the *Cleek*, an early iron, it will be realised by the collector that many makers were vying against each other to produce something unique, something which they could claim would hit the ball further.

We hear of today's irons having "the sweet spot" in the

A prize possession, a cleek used by W. Park Jnr.

A diamond-back cleek by Patrick of Leven. (Patrick started 1847).

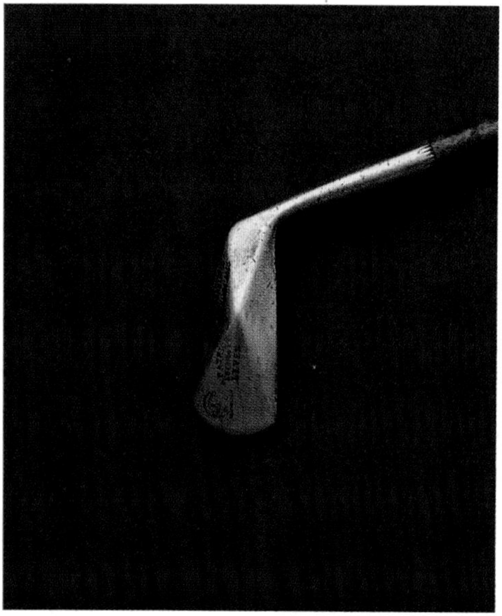

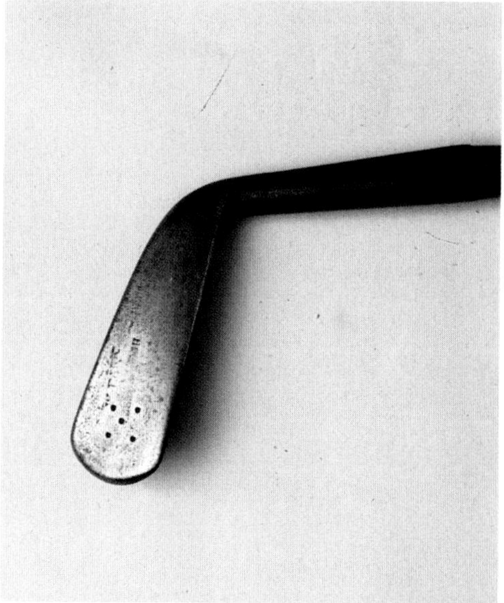

clubhead; surely they have imitated the models of the pre-1900's: a modern version of the diamond back; the round back; the pyramid back and the mussel back; all of these heads having the weight centred at a point on the back of the blade, directly behind the ball. Perhaps the clubs were *not* given a "swing weight", nor could torque (twist) be eliminated when the club was swung quickly, but a wooden-shafted club fitted with a good leather grip, gave a "feel" which the player – and the professional – knew was right in every way.

Within the range of cleeks the collector can find an infinite variety. The *driving cleek*, a club with very little loft; one of the earliest was a particularly nice diamond-backed club by A. Patrick of Leven. A model stamped A. Patrick Est.*1847* Leven, would be an exciting find.

The Long Driving Cleek. Titled the F. Murray driving cleek of about 1920 can be given a mention here. An advert by J. B. Halley & Company, London, states "this cleek is the only iron club of which it may be fairly said that it can beat the Brassie for distance". The head was forged by Hendry and Bishop, a narrow-bladed club with a "spliced iron socket to eliminate wrist jar"! A bishop's Mitre is the stamp of Hendry and Bishop.

The Lofting Cleek. I know these clubs are to be found with flat and rounded backs; and no doubt every iron maker during 1875 to 1890 was forging similar clubs with small variations. One club I

Niblick, rake iron and water iron for stream or bunker.

like is the short socket (through shaft) of 2½″, made for Carruthers, probably by Anderson of Anstruther. A nice parallel blade, heel to top of shaft 39½″.

The Rut Niblick. Undoubtedly the offspring of the Track iron. Similar in style to those mentioned, but with a larger head. It is deep at the neck end of the blade, a clumsy looking club, with strong socket. It has a thick shaft; length 38″ top to sole. A potential candidate for reshaping to a Track iron. Among the manufacturers look for Stewart, Anderson (St. Andrews), Condie and Winton.

The Mashie. One of the early irons which we are told was originally looked upon with trepidation. Yet after J. H. Taylor (winner of five Opens) proved it was a club for many purposes, a considerable number of professionals recommended it as an ideal club for a beginner, it having at that time the loft of a No. 5.

The name – Mashie – I have heard originated from the word "masher" or "Smasher", a club for smashing the ball from bad lies while getting distance. In a sense it replaced the lofting iron, with its head or face being shorter, it cut through longer grass more readily.

During the past few years we have seen more and more tournament professionals playing a No. 1 Iron off the tee, instead of the Driver. They invariably direct the ball more safely, sacrificing a little distance. The idea cannot be new, as at the turn

Mashies. From Driving-mashie to niblick, plus putting cleek.

of the century we had the *driving cleek*, *driving iron* and *driving mashie*, each with the approximate loft of a No. 1.

To the new collector it will probably come as a surprise to learn that there are so many different mashies; at least a dozen clubs for assorted shots.

Naming them, will suffice for the time being; their uses can be dealt with later. The approximate loft of each club will be in brackets.

I begin with the *Driving Mashie*, (a No. 1 iron), *Mashie Iron* (2/3), *Mashie Iron* (No. 3), *Mashie Cleek* (No. 4), *Standard* and *Long-faced Mashie* (No. 5), *Midget Mashie* (so stamped, but a full sized No. 5), *Deep-faced* and *Spade Mashie* (No. 6), *Taylors Mashie* (heavy No. 6), *Stymie Mashie* (No. 4/5), *Oval-faced Mashie Niblick* (No. 7), *Special "Square-faced" Mashie Niblick* (No. 7), and finally the *Water Mashie* (No. 5, 6 or 7, dependent upon the maker). Add a putter to this collection and one could play every shot he or she was confronted with – a set of clubs comprised of Mashies.

Before proceeding further I must also mention the "Maxwell" Mashie; it is certain to turn up, though it is a club of the early 1900's. Robert Maxwell thought of the idea of moving weight out of the socket of iron clubs by drilling holes through the socket sides. This necessitated extra weight in the sole of the club, so a flange was added or the base thickened up.

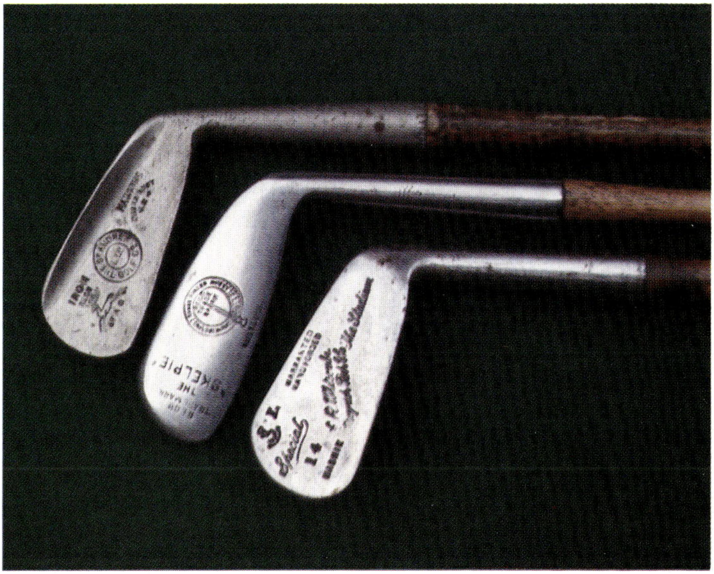

Well defined names and blacksmiths' stamps.

Many clubs of all types were made, cleeks, irons, mashies, niblicks, etc. and they sold well. The idea seemed right . . . the weight was behind the ball. However there had to be a snag; dampness and moisture entered the holes, the wood expanded when wet and contracted when dry, so the heads soon rattled. They were securely rivetted, but a loose socket means lack of power, so replacing shafts was commonplace. Certain cures were tried, candle-wax, cellulose and varnish; pitch (which melted as did the wax, on hot days – and what a mess the black tarry pitch made, particularly round the rim of the golf bag!) and wooden plugs glued into the socket holes. All to no avail.

Practical clubmakers, myself included, must have replaced dozens of hickory shafts in Maxwell irons.

Collectors will now presume that there are more mashies about than other irons; their guess is good, but putters must be leaders in the race. As I have previously stated, a collector can have great fun concentrating on only one type of club. These two types are tempting to the "small" collector.

Having detailed the approximate loft of the mashies, I can now describe their function.

The Driving Mashie. A No. 1 for directional tee shots, "long" short holes; keeping the ball low in the wind, or fine fairway lies. *Mashie Irons* 2 and 3 for similar use, particularly fairway play; and the *Mashie Cleek* No. 4 with a shallow face, getting good

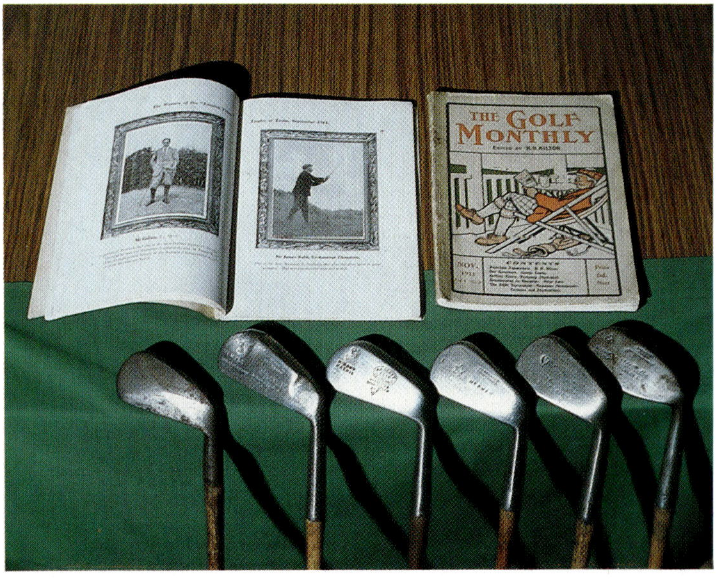

The back of the iron heads varied greatly.

height and little run.

The Standard and *Long-faced Mashie* gave plenty of lift from semi-rough as well as fairway lies and were ideal for the short holes of their time; many older players used them for the pitch and run shot around the green.

The Midget Mashie – akin to the No. 5 iron made for Scott of Elie, by Brodie & Son, Anstruther – has me baffled. I can only conclude it was named by a clubmaker with a sense of humour.

The Deep-faced and *Spade Mashie* are two of a kind. For use in heavier rough, sand trap shots, and particularly useful if the ball "sat high" off the fairway; the margin for error was lessened with the deep blade.

Taylor's Mashie. Five times Open Champion (and once beaten in a play-off for his sixth Championship) J. H. Taylor was the expert at the turn of the century with the mashie. He "manufactured" so many different shots with the club that he frequently played and scored well with only a handful of clubs in a small bag, his mashie taking care of the "short" game.

The Stymie Mashie. In matchplay golf, if a player's ball obstructed his opponent holing out, and providing the balls were not within 6″ of one another, this was a "stymie". If it were not possible to negotiate round the ball into the hole, the alternative was to loft the ball over, and though this could be done with clubs of varying degrees of loft, the stymie mashie was produced for the job. The stymie vanished in the early 1950's mainly due to a number of very important games and matches having been lost or won by the stymie rule. Here I think I shall start a crusade to have it returned for matchplay! It was one of the highlights of every great match of the late 1800's and early 1900's, history tells us.

The *Mashie Niblicks* were mainly for high lofting shots and strokes of short distance. Also for bunker play and removing the ball from coarse grass. A very popular club with all golfers. The *Oval Mashie Niblick* was regularly used on sandy links.

The *Water Mashie* (sometimes named the water iron). There was a variety of models with the blade having a loft of a No. 5 to No. 7. Some clubheads had the centre drilled out (a ⅝″ hole); others had up to six smaller holes in the blade; and there were clubheads with slots at the top of the blade; "rake-irons" which allowed the club easier passage when moving the ball out of water. These clubs were in use about the turn of the century and the arrival of the golf ball which floated must have played a part in their demise.

Before leaving the subject of the Mashie, I mention to

collectors that they will come across other NAMED Mashies. (I have written of Taylor's Mashie and Maxwell's Mashie). You will find the Tivoli Mashie, the Wemyss Mashie, the Celtic Mashie and the Fairlie Mashie too, but as they have related irons and Niblicks, they are another subject. The heads have characteristics of their own. Having mentioned the mashie niblick as

Various pitching clubs.

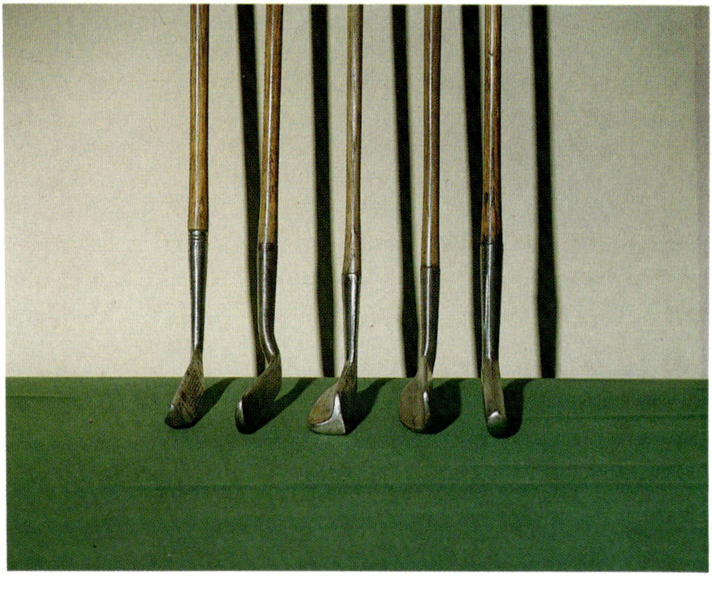

L/R. Chipper, Anti-shank putter, two flanged putters and 'Drainpipe' putter.

a lofting club and before writing of the putters, I must not overlook that great implement for pitching and bunker shots – the Niblick. This, the shortest of the iron clubs, and usually the heaviest, had the rough work to do when the ball was in deep trouble. The faces were deep, mostly oval in shape, and many designs were produced especially models with blades thin at the top and thick at the sole. It is a club easily recognised by the size of its head, which was very large.

Iron Putters.

In this instance the *straight-faced* clubs, as opposed to the older putting cleeks with loft and faces unmarked. These implements for use on the green come in many shapes and forms. The blade may range from the very shallow to the very deep. They may have a wry-neck, goose-neck, or swan-neck, each with varying degrees of bend in the base of the socket.

Willie Park Junior is acknowledged as having "invented" the wry-neck putter. The story goes that a putter fell off the pony and trap in which Park was riding; a wheel went over the putter socket, distorting it, but it seemed so nicely balanced and sat so well that in using it, Park's putting improved!

Putter sockets and shafts to collect may be oval or square; some round shafts being "bowed" as well as straight. The markings on the faces of the putters from around 1900 are equally fascinating too, with designs of great ingenuity; having been "punched", lined (scored) or "ringed", giving "grip" to the ball.

I reiterate, collecting *putters* by themselves, is a real novelty; seek out the different models, manufacturers' names and cleekmarks, and why not at some time take them out on the putting green and test them!

Incidentally, having written earlier of the stymie, and while on the subject of old putters; should the collector come across a putter which has two shallow saw cut rings round the shaft, (or two notches), the club has been marked deliberately. The marks will be 6″ apart and were a measure for satisfying and settling the arguments when a stymie situation arose. At a later date, when the folding score-card became fashionable, the marks on the shaft were dispensed with, the score-card being measured to the necessary 6″.

In trying to satisfy the demands of innovation, clubmakers produced numerous models of *putters*. Nicoll (cleek-mark a Hand) brought out the "Gem" as did many others later. Sayers produced the "Benny" (cleek-mark a Bird). Anderson and

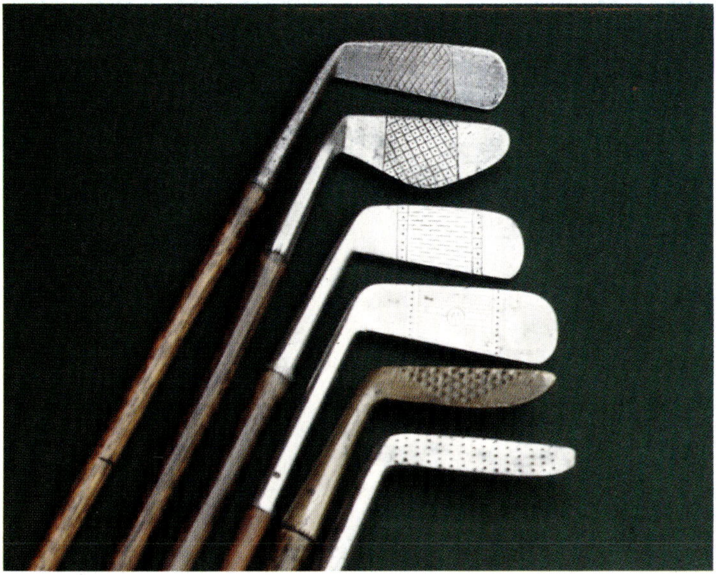

Assortment of putter heads.

NICOLL

LEVEN

Early Mark

Later Mark

NICOLL
LEVEN

F H AYRES

A & NCSL

Stewart and Spalding had an "Accurate" model. F. H. Ayres (their mark, a Maltese Cross), made a long shallow-faced putter, "The Sandwich". The Army & Navy Co-op (ANCLS) "The Holdfast", Anderson of St. Andrews designed "The Triumph" (the blade of the putter rising in pyramid fashion) and Hendry & Bishop produced "The Cardinal". Many other models could be named, but perhaps you will have more enjoyment finding them yourselves, particularly by the cleek-marks, of which you will be hearing more later.

Brass and gun-metal headed putters were fashionable too, including one by Bussey & Co. which had a head of brass and the socket part iron. The majority of the brass putters are smooth faced – indeed these straight-bladed clubs could be used left or right-handed – all of which appeared to have thick weighty heads. P. G. Allday & Co. Ltd. of Birmingham were the main suppliers of British brass-headed clubs from the 1890's; they too manufactured the brass sole plates for wooden clubs.

It seems a fair assumption that I have now given the would-be collector some information of the interesting and desirable items to be looking for. Clubs of many varieties in use to the turn of the century. The "third generation" (my way of grading them) which involves the mid-iron, push-iron, jigger, anti-shank and mammoth, etc. will, I trust, arouse even further the ambition to possess a worthwhile and valuable collection.

6. SOME SPECIALIST CLUBS

WITH the momentum of the popularity of the game continuing unabated, mass production manufacturers continued to turn out not only the standardised implements, but were shaping, styling and testing models which had to keep pace with the new techniques of the game. Understandably, this kept filling the golf bag with more and more clubs, each designed to play a part even if it was used only once during the course of a game. With this in mind, and having concluded the details of particular clubs to the turn of the century, I can proceed with other irons which, while being very functional, were sometimes at odds with one another.

Because they were invariably short-lived, they are desirables, so the Mid-iron, Push-iron, Jigger, Anti-Shank irons, Pitchers and Mammoth Niblicks can now be described for those who are new to collecting.

The Mid-Iron

A club of some 38″ in length, with the loft of a No. 2 iron, it was similar to the standard cleek, though slightly deeper and shorter in the blade. One could say that it ousted the cleek from the set.

The Push-Iron

An implement only for the better golfer. For playing low shots into the wind, or for seeking "run". This was a fairly straight-faced club, approximately 37″ long, used with plenty of "wrist-roll" instead of "follow-through" when the ball was struck. A good club for the windswept Scottish links. The name "push iron" will be stamped on the back of the blade; not every manufacturer made them.

The Jigger

The joker in the pack? A club of some 37″ with a narrow parallel blade. A twin to the approach cleek, but with a distinct upright lie. Like the club previously mentioned – the Push Iron – it was not an easy club to handle, but having a loft of between a No. 3 and No. 4, it was useful for playing out of the semi-rough and for "running-up" strokes. It was not a club for the hard fairways of seaside courses; the toe of the club so far off the ground was frightening. Most manufacturers produced a jigger, so there are a few to be found.

A mid-iron, push-iron, jigger and 3 anti-shank niblicks.

The Anti-Shank Irons

Actually the "anti-shank" design can apply to a set of irons, including the putter. The characteristics of the head and hosel are such that the ball cannot be sent off at an angle from the socket of the club.

The first of the two renowned designs emerged about 1892, Mr F. Fairlie shaping a club with the hosel in line with the top of the blade, i.e. the face was ahead of the shaft. About 3 years later Mr F. G. Smith produced a wry-neck model wherein the hosel is so "bent" at the base that the leading edge of the blade is also in advance of the shaft. Collectors will find Mashie Niblicks and Niblicks of this model made by Gibson (the "Star" cleek-mark), having upright flanges on the back, at the *toe* and *heel* of the club.

The principle of both of these designs is theoretically very sound, particularly in the shorter clubs, but they look rather unattractive, so have suffered a fate similar to the push-iron, jigger and cleeks (though they were in use into the 1930's) or perhaps one at least has been in hibernation. I gather an American company is now producing a copy of the Fairlie.

The Pitcher

Similar to the Chipper, with added loft. A short club, fairly upright in lie akin to the early putting cleeks. Used for shots of up to 80 yards from the flag. It could be used in two ways: one with open face adding cut and stop to the ball, the other with the "pitch and run" roll of the wrist. A safe club in a high wind.

The 'Skoogie' niblick or ('soup-ladle').

The Mammoth Niblick

Whosoever contributed this item to the range of clubs must have suffered not only agonies with his short game, but with bouts of insomnia. The Junior Mammoth – a Niblick – could only have followed a bad dream . . . ! The Giant Mammoth – unquestionably the culmination of a nightmare. The club is fashioned like a gargantuan niblick: it is a near-round, flat-bladed implement for use in bunkers, for lofting shots, and digging the ball out of deep rough. The Junior Mammoth has a 6″ blade, the Giant Mammoth something nearer to 8″ across. In silhouette it masquerades as a plate attached to a strong stick, and while it is much alike in length and weight to a Rut Niblick, there the similarity ends. Do buy the brute for your collection however, it will be a great "find".

While each of these clubs described *did* find a "home" in the set of clubs just after 1900, other hybrid specimens with interesting characteristics also showed face. As the last subject was the Niblick, I suggest you keep a sharp look-out for the Skoogee – or Skoogie – Mashie Niblick and Niblick.

Affectionately – though with some derision – it was known as the "soup-ladle", north of the border. A club with a fairly large blade, distinctly concave – sufficient to scoop a ball from a stream – and with a broad base which was well rounded: Gibson of Kinghorn being one of the manufacturers. Like many "oddities", it had a very restricted life, a player was able to strike the ball twice during the action of one stroke, when it was hit "thin".

Other irons included the ribbed-faced blade, with grooves from toe to heel about 1/8″ deep and wide. It gave backspin and was guaranteed to remove all paint from the ball. The double-faced chipper; for playing right and left-hand shots.

W. Park Jnr took out a patent for a step-faced (yes, step) lofting iron; another club which contributed to restrictions being put on the depth and width of grooves on the clubface.

Putters, too, entered this arena. Forgan's "drainpipe"; a club with the head being a right-angled extension of the socket; round and shallow in the blade and useful enough for putting on fast greens. Putters were fashioned with varying L-shaped flanges while others were grooved in the sole.

A 'ribbed' faced mashie. It was made illegal due to the depth and width of the grooves.

Aluminium putters with assorted lines and signs, lumps and bumps as a direction finder or for gauging the line of the stroke; all of which were legal. Many failed to catch the imagination of the user, however, so gradually faded from the scene. Perhaps I am safe in saying that putters did invent fear.

In describing a fair number of the iron clubs to look for in collecting, I have touched on only a handful of the many blacksmiths' stamps or cleek-marks, which keep in step, as near as possible, with the clubs of each period. I also stated that just after the turn of the century, (from about 1908 to 1912) the number of cleekmakers dwindled quickly, due to the larger factories increasing their output and using drop-forging methods as opposed to hand forging. While the major concerns had their own stamps, individual professionals wanted their symbol too, so the number of "marks" grew rather than diminished.

Furthermore, some of those larger manufacturers were using additional, and/or redesigned stamps, so companies such as Spalding, Stewart, Forgan and Gibson, who were – with other firms – supplying iron clubs, or iron heads to the professional, understandably held numerous stamps to fulfil their orders.

It is important that as collectors unearth "new" marks, (or makers' names), they have some idea of their originations. There were many smiths hand forging – and drop-forging – cleeks, irons, mashies, niblicks and putting cleeks at the turn of the

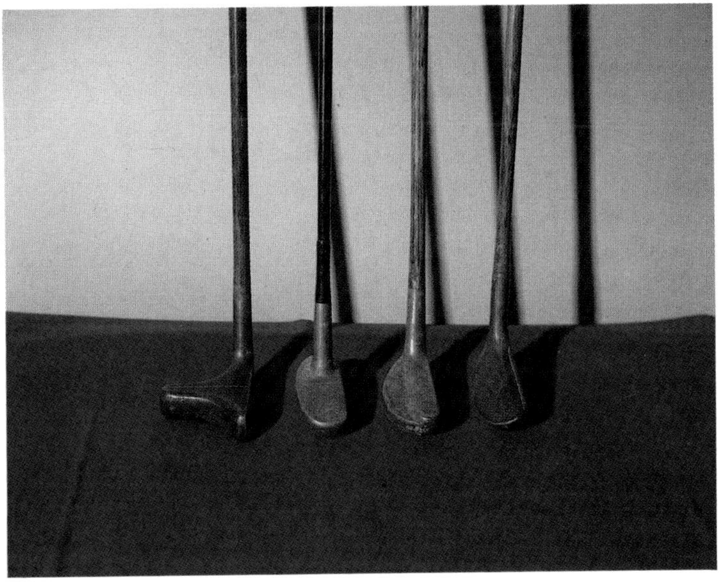

Various models of Aluminium putters.

century, so symbols on the irons were commonplace. It is surprising that so few of these makers advertised their brands in these times; either it was a costly business via the magazines or periodicals, or they were sufficiently reliant on personal recommendation to keep their stock turning over.

Researching the history of the old "cleek-marks" it has to be said that the task is not an easy one. Interesting and enlightening it may be, but frustrating too as little documentation is available and the generations that were involved are passing on. Permit me to present one example; the name of Anderson and their

associations with clubmaking. You will frequently come across their stamps.

An early generation of clubmakers was D. Anderson & Sons, St. Andrews.

("D" had five sons.)

James Anderson & Sons, (son of "D") opened in St. Andrews.

James Anderson (grandson of "D") went into partnership with D. Blyth as Anderson & Blyth, St. Andrews. Anderson & Gourlay together in St. Andrews.

Robert Anderson & Sons in business in Edinburgh.

James Anderson & Son, Clubmakers in Anstruther.

Alex Anderson, Clubmakers in Anstruther. Not related to the St. Andrews family.

Anderson Rubber Co. in Edinburgh, were advertising in 1898.

Anderson, Anderson & Anderson, Queen Victoria Street, London. Completes (perhaps) a galaxy of individuals of whom it must be said cumulatively must have had a tremendous knowledge of the trade.

AAA

As to the marks on their clubs. The St. Andrews Andersons had name stamps only, as did the Edinburgh companies. Anderson of Anstruther used single and double rings with their name inscribed therein (the double ring having a dash-dot-dash centre). An arrow was the mark used by the second Anstruther factory. Andersons of London have an elaborate design with two hemispheres, a banner, the lion and the unicorn, and flags making their symbol. Incidentally, one of the clubs sold by Anderson of Edinburgh, has within the oval name stamp the lettering "LOTSIRB". I cannot trace their having a shop or works in Bristol, but suspect there is a connection. Hang on to one of those so stamped clubs for interest value. Anderson and Gourlay's mark was the initials entwined.

ST. ANDREWS ANSTRUTHER

Anderson & Gourlay St. Andrews

The Gourlay family also had many roots – or branches – they had a variety of blacksmiths' stamps, particularly as one of the family teamed up with Spence of St. Andrews. James Gourlay & Son were in business in Carnoustie: their cleek-marks were a crescent moon with a star and a crescent moon with a planet. Later they had an anchor which varied in style dependent on the maker who cut the stamp, a rope being added to one anchor.

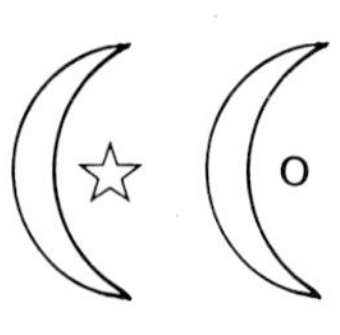

In St. Andrews, Spence and Spence were in business in a small way, and one of the Gourlays joined the company to trade as Spence & Gourlay. Their marks were an Anchor with an "S" entwined also a clover leaf – with or without stalk, their initials in the leaves. Forgan took over the business in St. Andrews, but

Gourlay continued in Carnoustie to the mid 1930's.

The collector will glean from these illustrations how involved the subject is, cleekmaking ran a difficult course with many hazards. However it gives great enjoyment seeking out the marks.

Before proceeding further with blacksmiths' marks, I will conclude an item with which I was dealing earlier; that of irons which were autographed, designed or named after a person well involved with the game.

I have described the clubs of R. Maxwell, J. H. Taylor, F. Fairlie and F. G. Smith. Others worth collecting are those with the autograph of Open champions, James Braid, Geo. Duncan, Edward Ray, H. Vardon, A. Herd, J. White and A. Simpson (twice runner-up in the Open) well defined. R. H. Montmorency, an amateur of note, overstamped many irons (by Gibson) as, I believe, did F. G. Tait, (by Nicoll).

Certain patentees had their ideas accepted, probably the best known of these being Hugh Logan – a clubmaker who had "itchy feet", moving from one firm to another. He designed the "Genii" Model while with Wm. Gibson of Kinghorn, and many of his clubs can be found throughout the country. Another named club was the "Wemyss" model; a nicely shaped iron with the toe and the heel of the blade thinned down (on the back of the club) leaving a thickened part directly behind the ball. The "Oggmented" Iron, by William Ogg had about 1″ of the toe of the long irons thickened – on the back of the blade – giving added weight which was a prevention against torque opening the face of the club on impact with the ball.

The "Huntley" aluminium headed putter – with a rounded sole – was fitted with a specially designed hickory shaft. The "grip" area was thick enough to dispense with the leather or "rubberised" covering, but it was distinctly grooved or gouged to accept a positioning of the thumbs in direct line with the toe of the club. One or two conventional putters also have this shaft fitted; they are all collectable.

Other rarities are the Dunlewy model clubs; woods and irons having a sharp "V" shaped sole. The wood clubs sit nicely on the fairway; the irons – particularly on hard ground – required firm gripping to avoid error. The niblick, a cruel looking implement must have been the ideal club to expose the rubber interior of a golf ball should a player top the shot; the outer cover would not withstand the hatchet blow this club could deliver.

The "Scuffler" is a novel addition to a collection; many made

GOURLEY

SPENCE & GOURLEY

C. GIBSON

by Spence & Gourlay are jigger shaped clubs; shorter in the shaft akin to a putter. (Some are stamped "approach putter"). The blade ⅝″ in depth, ⅜″ at the top and approx. ¾″ on the sole. Clubs obviously made for flat seaside links.

Probably the doyen of all, however, was R. L. Urquhart, who

The "Dunlewy" 'V'-sole spoon and niblick.

took out numerous patents, each relating to the irons with adjustable heads. Most of the clubs had cogs and ratchets which could be locked in position with a screw or key. This was the lazy man's club, the loft could be adjusted from driving iron to niblick. Regretably the birth of these clubs was premature, they were patented in the mid 1890's when the "rock hard" gutty ball was in use. A pity Urquhart had not known the rubber-cored ball was only a few years away. For your interest, I played a few holes in the 1930's with an Urquhart patent; the blade was pulled out of the cogged socket, then locked at the club "heel" with a screw. Using a *modern* (1930's) ball, it was quite an experience, every shot felt as if the clubhead was contacting stone and most long shots had the fingers tingling. The noise at impact was disconcerting too. Pitch shots were easier, from mashie loft to niblick, the slightly rounded sole biting the sandy fairways more readily, and by chance rather than skill the ball did stop fairly quickly. If the clubs never really won favour with golfers in the early days, they were certainly frowned upon by the greenkeepers; the green

was meant for a putter not a makeshift driving iron, which the club became when the face was straightened. Mr Urquhart (aided by his family) left us much of interest, however, and collectors the world over can continue to look out for those real curios.

'The Urquhart' adjustable headed iron of the late 1890s and 'The Whole in One' adjustable iron of the 1920s.

Another view of the above.

Many other fascinating specimens for the golfer "came off the drawing board" between 1890 and 1920, but I will not get involved with them until I have given further details of the cleek-marks and the true irons we want in our collection.

It was a curious thing that – as records show – many of the old manufacturers who stamped iron heads went out of business about the same time; makers such as Crighton, Premier, Harrower, British Golf Co., Stirling & Gibson, Fleming & Barry, Wilson and Winton to name but a few. However, immediately prior to and after the 1914/18 war, new companies sprang to life, with the premises and machinery of older ones being resurrected or taken over. They obviously had the foresight that, following the war, recreation was going to be of paramount importance. Industry was slowly finding its feet and the demand for golf clubs had found its niche. Iron and steel were in short supply, but out of every crisis will emerge something tangible, so the metal for the heads duly appeared.

U

Urquhart

BG CO.

British Golf Co. London Ltd.

A.G. SPALDING & BROS.

HAMMER FORGED

Having taken an "in depth" look at the cleek-marks of the Andersons and Gourlays, I realise there are a few things which may still puzzle the new collector, so I take this opportunity to tidy them up.

The word SPECIAL will be found on countless clubs; every other head maker owned one of these stamps, and whether the implement was mediocre or marvellous the stamping would be there. Do not be pressured by any club seller into paying extra for this marking.

Iron heads which are stamped with a capital "L" are ladies (or lighter) clubs. They will have an overall difference in length and weight, and in many instances the "grips" will be thinner. The stamping made its appearance around 1905 and may be seen on irons, including the putter.

As I have emphasised earlier, it is very necessary to inspect or scrutinise the markings, names and wording on the clubhead – also watch the face of the blade for variations – they can differ greatly. For instance the Spalding Bros. details can be missed or overlooked. The Anvil stamp of this company comes in two styles, as will be seen from the sketches shown; the older clubs have the cone of the anvil below the main flat surface; the later irons have the stamp with a level top. The Spalding hammer mark differs too; some blades are stamped "hand-forged", while others have the wording "hammer-forged", the latter, particularly the Crescent Moon putter, often having "made in England" stamped on the base or sole, it being manufactured in their London factory.

I will later name some of the manufacturers who, whether by accident or design, altered – or twinned – their stamps, and will also list some professionals – who did not make iron heads – but had symbols which signified their ideas or authority involving a particular model.

7. THEY MADE THEIR MARK

ALTHOUGH there is much still to be written regarding the numerous old bona-fide clubs, as well as those which were innovative but short-lived, I am now getting into what I termed the fourth (and final) generation of implements, which complete those wooden shafted irons up to around 1920. This was an era when the clubs were being given numbers, firstly stamped on the back of the blade, later on the sole. I clarify a point here by mentioning that numerous irons, particularly putters, have a patent or reference number as an indication of their manufacture. As examples, R. Forgan & Son, St. Andrews, marked many middle irons with anything from 10 to 100; Winton of Montrose using, in my experience, 1 to 41. I understand these were generally model or batch numbers, but they are of little relevance as I fear you will not collect a full "set" 1 to 100.

First workshop of John Letters (1919). Note the stone slab floor with 'standing' blocks of wood.

Regarding the numbering which indicated the loft of the club, the matter is more straightforward. The early clubs, after 1912, had a number 1 on the driving irons, the number 2 or 3 could appear on a blade stamped "iron" or "mid-iron" and the collector can find clubs by Winton of Montrose (cleek-mark a diamond) with a 5 or a V on their mashies. Anderson had a swan-neck putter with a reference of some five or six numbers. J. B. Halley & Co. Ltd. who took over Anstruther Golf Irons Ltd., had 2A and 3A numbers on certain models. From my own observation, having tested the angle of the clubface, I surmise this classification indicated a more generous degree of loft, in other words it could have been 2¼ or 2½. At any rate the numbering was an indication that the names – cleek, jigger, mashie and niblick – were on their way out, and that manufacturers were becoming increasingly sophisticated by designing the clubface to give the golf ball a precise trajectory, which until then had been calculated guesswork.

By 1925, wooden shafted clubs were not just "looking over their shoulder" at the slender steel shafts which the U.S.A. had legalised for tournament play, they were seeing the "stainless" and rustless clubs, in matched sets, each being numbered on the sole, shining brightly in the bag. This, truly, was the end of an era. Wood shafts had been used for centuries, but it was inevitable they would go, for not only was hickory becoming more difficult to obtain, as an import, it was costly. Steel shafts had a longer life, the shafts stood up to the harder hitting of the ball, virtually eliminated torque and, of course, it gave British industry the chance to fill the wants of clubmakers.

I will go no further into the matter of steel shafts. As I stated, the information imparted would embrace wooden shafts and clubs which were non-rustless. However, there is a related matter which *does* require a mention; that of older irons which were not expected to rust.

Let us look back to the very first iron-headed clubs used in Britain. We know not where or who fashioned them, but it is known that Lanarkshire and its surrounds were the areas which "housed" the largest iron producing works. The valleys of the Clyde and Forth could supply the more common "earthy" matters for smelting which were "clay-band" and "black-band" stone. (I wonder if the upper area of the Firth of Forth, with its coal dusted sand, was the supplier of the ore ingredient from which Waverley metal originated – the metal from which many of Park's clubs were made; a greyer speckled iron. I shall be happy

Forging iron heads. Note the moulds on bench. Anstruther Golf Irons Ltd (J. B. Halley & Co. Ltd.)

to be informed. I am only guessing!) Originally the iron was colloquially known as "pig-iron", but with its various processes and its added haematites and oxides, purer iron and steel were formed. This was followed by "rust proofing", and the many original efforts made to keep a clubhead polished were noble indeed.

Throughout my reading and researching, I have been unable to determine a precise date when the first head was coated to prevent rust. The venerable clubmakers and historians known to me are of the opinion that it was just prior to the turn of the century that "tinning" first took place; that is, the clubs were plated or dipped in liquified tin or tin compound. Collectors will discover more than one type of coating on the blade, this being determined by whosoever finished off the head. The name SHERARDIZED will be found on a number of irons, clubs made just after 1900. It is thought that a Mr Sherard was the patentee, he "dipped" the club in what must have been too light a coating, as rust fairly quickly tarnished his work. Later attempts at keeping the ravages of dampness at bay did bring

T. MORRIS
ST. ANDREWS

Pre 1900

After 1901

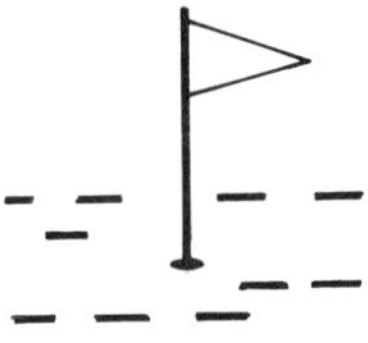

R. FORGAN & SON

improvements, (1912 by the Norusta Golf Co. Shandwick Place, Edinburgh) and around 1920 the metal of the head was being stamped stainless. This did not entirely solve the problem either, as the moisture, particularly of seaside courses, ate its way into the metal. Caddies of those bygone days had not been wholly relieved of one of their chores, a piece of emery cloth was still one of the tools of their trade.

Anyway, should the collector desire a curio in various irons, I think it worthwhile giving room to an early "coated" implement.

I have already explained – and shown – how one or two makers had more than one symbol; or had modifications made to the original.

The name of Tom Morris of St. Andrews stands out among the great names in golf. His early clubs were stamped TOM MORRIS in capital letters, superseded by the name in script. Tom Morris Jnr in script was on a few clubs, but they are rare. Collectors can keep a sharp eye open for T. MORRIS woods with ST. ANDREAN under the name. Also on the hickory shaft, just below the grip, the bearded face of Old Tom is stamped. Equally exciting, find a club – wooden head – with the same features printed in coloured transfer form, clubs of the period following the 1918 war.

Unlike Tom Morris's shop which still looks down upon the last green at St. Andrews, the name of Forgan has disappeared. Robert Forgan was a nephew of Hugh Philp. They formed a partnership in the mid 1850's wherein very rare and collectable spliced clubs – mainly putters – were dual-stamped Philp/Forgan. Collectors who find this relic (beware of the fake!) are fortunate indeed.

Robert Forgan was one of the more shrewd and astute clubmakers from the period of the 1850's, he was acknowledged as the first person to secure the rams horn in driver-heads with wood pegs at an inward slant. He also has a claim to the symmetrical hand-hammering of gutta balls. In conjunction with Tom Morris, Robert Forgan was accredited with the bulk-buying of hickory for shafts, enabling lower prices to be agreed upon. In 1863 he was appointed clubmaker to the Prince of Wales, receiving permission to stamp all clubs with the three ostrich plumes. In 1901 following the death of Queen Victoria, R. Forgan (who had by 1881, been joined by his son) was able to convert his stamp to the Royal Crown, and it is those clubs which collectors should have with their other acquisitions.

The Prince of Wales feathers stamp is a must in the "set" but do, if possible, buy from a reliable source or have the clubs authenticated, as some are given an 1870 date when it could be 1890. The position of the "feathers" stamped on the club blade may vary; this was due to Forgan having an outside source manufacture the iron head. One can look upon this as being a "false" mark, but in effect it is a genuine club. Readers may recall I stated earlier that iron heads were supplied in a sub-contracted fashion.

It is of interest that Forgan did not manufacture iron heads until late in the 19th century, he purchased them from another famous St. Andrews firm, that of Tom Stewart. Here, again, it is regrettable that another name and symbol disappeared from the golfing scene. "Pipe brand" clubs made by Stewart were spread throughout the golfing world, which is proven by the number of irons regularly unearthed. Tom Stewart's early cleek-mark was a simple clay-pipe, with a slightly curved stem. A later mark in the early 1900's the lettering "T.S.St.A.Reg.Trade Mark" was stamped below a straighter-stemmed pipe, which also had a larger bowl. Another early Stewart mark was that of a zig-zag line; occasionally it was snake-like.

T. STEWART
Old Mark

For the befit of the new collectors I will back-pedal for a moment to the Forgan and Morris fraternity. Clubs with the name A. Forgan, Glasgow, younger brother of Robert Forgan (his cleek-mark the pear tree from the Glasgow City coat of arms) are nice additions to "the hoard"; they are scarce (iron heads made by Tom Stewart) but worth parting with a few extra pounds if clearly stamped.

T. S. St. A.
Reg. Trade Mark
New Mark

Jack Morris clubs (he was the nephew of Old Tom Morris and first "professional" to the Hoylake Golf Club), are also desirables; they too will command a premium. They are stamped name and club address.

T. STEWART

Here, I think, is an appropriate moment to illustrate further the importance of St. Andrews as the hub of the club-making industry – no disrespect to the neighbouring satellite towns of Anstruther, Leven and Kinghorn.

T. STEWART

History has it that business thrives on competition. St. Andrews being graced by a renowned University probably coined such a phrase. It must be that by the Grace of God and good fortune there was land in which golf courses were not made or designed, but were natural; the townsfolk turned their hands to making the Royal and Ancient game what it is today. However, from the second half of the 19th century to 1920 clubmakers thrived in the area and many tons of iron and steel

**A. FORGAN
GLASGOW**

COLLECTING OLD GOLFING CLUBS

D + W AUCHTERLONIE ST. ANDREWS

TOM AUCHTERLONIE & SON

ST. ANDREWS GOLF CO.

ST. ANDREWS GOLF CO

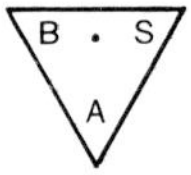

BRODIE & SONS ANSTRUTHER

R. CONDIE ST. ANDREWS

BRODIE & CO. ANSTRUTHER

must have been delivered to the host of cleekmakers in the town.

Looking through old catalogues and at the advertisements of these early days is a pleasurable pastime; the information is clear and to the point; there is an old-fashioned charm in the efforts to detail the superiority of particular clubs and, of course, from 1910 up to the late 1920's, there were many clubmaking competitions to enter, with the major prize-winners putting their wares on exhibition.

R. Condie & Sons, with a rose as their symbol, was another of the great iron producers of St. Andrews. They advertised as "Golf Cleek and Iron Specialists". "All heads hand-forged and guaranteed". With a tit-bit "American and Colonial orders a Speciality" boldly printed in their advert.

Incidentally in 1910 T. Stewart (Pipe brand) stated in their advertising "No cast iron or drop forged heads sold, all hand forged". Such claims had to be accurate!

Anderson & Blyth (mentioned previously), in the same city, must have pleased Stewart by stating *they* sold the famous Pipe brand models. Which all goes to confirm a written comment in 1912 that "trade relationships have been placed not only on a controlled footing, but the foundation will have been laid for a better understanding among the makers . . . the makers know their trade and interests, let the cleekmakers stick together, if they do not they will speedily hang together"!

Still in St. Andrews is a name synonymous with the city and of golf; that of Auchterlonie. David and William Auchterlonie (Willie – Open champion in 1893) were in business together in the early 1890's, specialising in patenting and copying clubs of all types. William's son, Laurie, also a legend in clubmaking, still resides in the city, beside his shop which exudes wonderful smells of varnish, wood, leather and glue. It is universally recognised that what Laurie doesn't know of the Royal and Ancient game, its personalities and the equipment of yesteryear and today, is of no consequence.

Just a putt away, clubs, bags, umbrellas, golf balls and golf clothing fill the premises of Tom Auchterlonie & Son. Son Eric – aided and abetted by Jim Horsfield – expert clubmakers in their own right, are short of nothing connected with the game. Neither company has cleek-marks, the name stamp is the hallmark of the continuation of craftsmanship.

For collectors who are mainly interested in the cleek-marks on irons I must not overlook a fine stamping of the St. Andrews Golf Co., St. Andrews. Many clubs are plated or stainless, though hickory shafted. The smith's stamp is of a leaping stag. A very collectable club at an inexpensive price.

Leaving St. Andrews, I move round the coast to Anstruther, another small town renowned for iron heads: produced by the Andersons (marks previously shown); Brodie (cleek-mark B); Brodie & Son, (a shield with B. & S. A. within). The small factory, Anstruther Golf Irons Ltd., was taken over by J. B. Halley & Co. Ltd.

THE  SCOT

NICOLL OF LEVEN

Onwards to Leven, where the "hand of friendship", the famous symbol of Nicoll of Leven was hammered on hundreds of thousands of heads for over a century. Alas the factory is vacant now.

W. GIBSON & CO. LTD KINGHORN

Progressing westward to the area of a star now extinct, home of William Gibson of Kinghorn, probably the most prolific manufacturer of clubs in the Kingdom of Fife. A five-pointed star was his cleek-mark. He had trained in Anstruther under the watchful eye of J. Anderson, but motivation, inspiration and ambition drove him to innovation: clubs, particularly irons of new shape, style and design emerged from his numerous forges. He built up a business which has left for collectors, samples of great variety and interest. Perhaps it would be remiss of me if I omitted the name of Hugh Logan at this time. A member of Gibson's staff who was a genius in machine work and in design; he will be remembered at least for his Genii model. He should undoubtedly have had his own business, but whatever the circumstances, he did not, so moved from one company to another – even to representing a golf ball manufacturer – seeking fame and fortune. Fortune did not favour him when he became manager of F. A. Johnston of London; it collapsed – through no fault of Logan's – within a year of his appointment. Along with the Genii model, Logan's bent-neck irons and an apparatus for teaching the "correct" golf swing, will not be forgotten.

M. BINGHAM

'CLINGER' MODEL by Gibson

Another small firm existed in Kinghorn about 1910. I regret I have little knowledge of it, other than that their irons were stamped in an oval shaped ring FIFE KINGHORN GOLF CO.

FIFE KINGHORN GOLF CO

Still in the county of Fife in which, in the early 1900's, at least 90% of the Scottish cleekmakers had their roots, I must not overlook the "minnows" of the trade.

T. Nicholson of Pittenweem produced iron heads, but I suspect this was a part-time job in the trade of being a blacksmith. His business was taken over by T. A. Galloway, who was forging irons in 1890.

T. NICHOLSON

I must also mention A. H. Scott of Elie, because of his

cleek-marks which will be found on various irons. He was a very fine maker of wood clubs, but he bought his iron heads from St. Andrews and Anstruther. His stamps grew in size and stature. Because of his association with the Connaught family – teaching and supplying them with equipment – he was appointed clubmaker to King George V, so was able to sport a three-tiered symbol. A four-pointed star supporting a crown, with a lion on top. Some of Scott's irons are stamped without the star, others with the star and crown missing – leaving the lion as the single mark. Another hammer brand stamp has recently been discovered. In 1909 Johnstone Bros. of Tayport, Fife were forging iron heads. Their advert is shown.

Scott of Elie (Fife)

Collectors will find sketches of a number of the cleek-marks which relate to the manufacturers quoted. Shortly I will deal with the companies which were in the business north of the Firth of Tay – primarily Carnoustie – also with the more isolated firms in the Lothians and eastern seaboard of Scotland. I then intend to show the marks which relate to England, followed by the personalised stamps of professionals and sports stores who bought in their irons.

Furthermore, it is worth recording that a number of cleek-marks emanated from the Professional Golfers' Co-operative Association warehouses; most of these were from around 1920, but when a collector discovers an iron with the symbol such as a lion rampant, an archer with bow and arrow; the head of Punch; the clubs were lower priced implements, supplied to the P.G.C.A., by such firms as Ayres, Spalding, Gibson and Nicoll. Golf professionals at the smaller courses (9-hole, or short 18) who were members of the Professional Golfers' Association were happy to have the facility to order single items or single sets from their co-operative.

P G C A
LION BRAND

Before I leave the county of Fife, I would like to say that it was great fun at an auction (golf session) in St. Andrews in May last, (1984). Along with the Jackson (Perth) baffing spoon, which was sold for £2000, one white painted "feathery" golf ball was "knocked down" for £750 and another, nameless, for £580. It shows the *relics* are really in demand.

HAMMER BRAND

Johnstone Bros
Tayport

For the new collector, though, I saw numerous "lots" of clubs going for reasonable prices. Fourteen hickory irons for £48. Sixteen wooden shafted irons for £65, 20 various at £45, and 15 hickory woods at £45. For the time being forget the scare-headed bulger driver fetching £150 or 4 ditto realising £230. If you reside within travelling distance of companies auctioning golf equipment, it might be an interesting and a profitable journey.

8. AWAY FROM THE KINGDOM OF FIFE

HAVING written of the well-known Scottish iron club manufacturers located in the county of Fife, I can now travel further afield.

A number of well established makers were dotted around the country and they persevered valiantly until the first World War began. They were well scattered however, so covering the remainder of Scotland is a relatively simple task.

North of the Firth of Tay lies the famous championship course of Carnoustie; home of a number of cleekmakers who vied with one another to fulfil the demands of the increasing trade. Gourlay (his crescent moons and his anchors were described earlier) was probably the better known of iron forgers. W. Hewitt, identifying his work with the mark of a heart with an arrow across it, was in business in a smaller way; as was Charles Brand, whose stamp – similar to a P.G.C.A. mark – has been shown as the Lion rampant. A club from W. Craigie of Carnoustie, recognisable by a gun (rifle-shaped), is a very collectable item; they are difficult to find. Cochrane of the same town sold their irons with the mark of a rope fashioned to a loose reef knot. T. Harrower – a heart stamp – felt the pressures of the larger manufacturers and was eventually taken over by Cochrane in 1913. Crighton Ltd., also cleekmakers, were in business in the town until they closed in mid-1912.

Just over 20 miles north of Carnoustie lie two more fine seaside courses in the town of Montrose. The name Winton of Montrose was synonymous with high class workmanship. Father and soon ran the factory, embossing their iron heads with a diamond, and many of their clubs are to be found both North and South of the Border. The firm was taken over by A. M. Pirie & Son of Glasgow who used the diamond as one of the models in their range.

While it is supposed that in the golfing areas above Montrose: e.g. Aberdeen, Nairn and Dornoch – there may have been smiths turning out various iron heads, documentation indicates the clubmakers of these parts were shaping *wooden* headed implements and golf balls.

However, one name up there *does* interest me. That of Weir of

W. HEWITT
CARNOUSTIE

C. Brand Carnoustie

J. & W. CRAIGIE
CARNOUSTIE

COCHRANE
CARNOUSTIE

T. Harrower
Carnoustie

J. WINTON
MONTROSE

Cruden Bay. In view of the fact that early cleekmakers stamped their irons with their name and address in an oval style and added the word MAKER between the two, the old clubs I possess, marked with his name, give me food for thought. I wonder if Weir or a local smith was, in fact, making a few iron heads. Being well away from the manufacturers further South, it might have paid him to have some forged locally! A task for the winter months if nothing else.

HAND FORGED

MADE IN SCOTLAND

Returning from the North, I cannot ignore the "Fair City of Perth", where golf has been played for centuries and may even dispute some of the claims made by Fife and the Lothians. Certainly balls and wood-headed clubs were made there. The names of Jackson (born in 1805) whose clubs are rare and expensive; also Lang and McDonald – of whom I know little other than from trade directories – turned out implements of wood which are much sought after by connoisseurs.

REGD.

GLASGOW GOLF CO.

South to Glasgow where the firm, Premier Golf Company, was turning out nice models, particularly the Pitcher, with a curved sole. Their mark is a line of three small "crowns".

The Glasgow Golf Company, with a Thistle as their symbol was, after the first World War, turning out non-rustless and rustless heads. The clubs, though scarce, have not a great value on them as yet.

PREMIER GOLF CO.

Another name with longer lasting impact was that of John Letters. In a small lean-to shed the firm began clubmaking in 1919, and from that time never looked back. Their irons were (and are) admired by professionals and amateurs alike, and span the world. John Letters in early days used the Swilcan Bridge as a symbol.

Across country to the Lothians (Edinburgh and district, which was at one time Midlothian, adjoined East Lothian), where I hazard a guess there were/are more golf courses within hailing distance of each other, than anywhere on earth.

At this time I will embody Leith, Musselburgh, Bruntsfield and Edinburgh as one: they are representative of Midlothian, an area of some 15 miles radius.

As this book is primarily for the "beginner collector", here I seek the indulgence of the established collector to enable me to inform the newcomer, and those not acquainted with the "birthplaces" of the game, on how particular areas confirm our recognition of golf being a Scottish pastime.

The Leith and Musselburgh links are sited on the shores of the Firth of Forth; Bruntsfield links are, to all intents and purposes, in the heart of Edinburgh. Golf – albeit in its infancy – was played on the sandy grass in the dock areas of Leith; a few miles eastward similar activities were taking place in Musselburgh.

As Leith and Bruntsfield were more central to the city, the merchants, professional men and others of high rank and society found easier access from their businesses to these areas; but visualise the congestion and confusion as donkey cart, pony trap and, later, the Hansom cab, all converged with those on foot, to find a spot on the tee.

With the arrival of the horse-drawn omnibus, small groups, associations and societies, habitues of the Bruntsfield Links, gathered at focal points and were driven to the city outskirts to play on Musselburgh links which, by that time, was a superior and longer course – superior in yardage and by one hole! Eventually Musselburgh links housed many prominent clubs, some of which had been granted regal favour, and appended the title Royal to their name. Royal Burgess – possibly an offshoot of The Bruntsfield Links Golf Club – Royal Musselburgh, and The Honourable Company of Edinburgh Golfers (who had departed Leith links) – each had clubhouses there.

Cochrane
Edinburgh

Alas, through lack of foresight, Musselburgh links (9 holes) is only a ghostly shadow of its former self. The clubs that made it famous moved away to design and lay out their own courses and links – and a wonderful job they made of them too! Royal Burgess, Royal Musselburgh and Muirfield – the latter being one of the great courses of the world – and left behind a race-course/golf course of uncertain future. To the Musselburgh Golf Heritage which is striving to retain a bit of the past, may I say I wish you every success, history at least is supporting you well.

STIRLING & GIBSON
CLEEK & IRON MAKERS
JORDAN LANE
EDINBURGH

So having devoted some attention to the early Lothian links around Edinburgh where, in the early 18th century, the game was being treated with increasing seriousness, I return to the implements of play. I think I agree with the theorists' notion that this area is "how and where it all began".

One of the yet unsolved mysteries regarding the game is that concerning the first "Keeper of the Green" (professional); we cannot put a name to the first maker of a play-club or an iron, though ball-makers were named in the 1500's. What we do know, however, is that beside Bruntsfield Links there lived a James McEwan (born 1747) who was firstly a carpenter, then a clubmaker. It is reputed that McEwan made long wooden-headed clubs stamped with his name and the design of a thistle. This, I suggest, was the first indication of a clubmaker having his own motif, which would be for identification as much as for decoration. The course having been in existence in the early 1700's would, by the 1770's, require permanent supervision, so why not James McEwan? Towards the end of the century Douglas Gourlay, a maker of feathery golf balls, arrived in the area, and for the benefit of players on the links shared the same workshop with McEwan. Together they must have been a great draw to the links: equipment and repairers were within reach. They too, like the Societies founded there, eventually moved down to Musselburgh.

C. DAVIDSON
MUSSELBURGH

So Musselburgh Links, on fine seaside grass, attracting the wealthy and better players to its facilities and natural qualities, enticed not only golfers, but a host of clubmakers and ball-makers to settle there as well. Mr George Colville, the Musselburgh Golf Historian, has informed me that in his young days – just after the turn of the century – there were 29 Artisan clubs in addition to the private clubs using the links.

McEWAN
MUSSELBURGH

Expansion of such enormity kept all of the equipment supplies busy for many years and the clubs they made, wood and iron, are all great finds for the collector.

It would appear that only the cleek-marks of Carrick and Davidson originated in Musselburgh – although D. McEwan irons, stamped by Condie and Forgan, are to be found – the Lothians, for one reason or another, apparently did not have the desires of Fife to symbolise their workmanship.

W. PARK

The very early stamping by McEwan was in straight-forward capital letters McEWAN; later, particularly on irons, the name MUSSELBURGH was added.

W. PARK & SON

William Park, always know as Willie, had his premises at the same links. He branded his clubs with W. PARK and W. PARK MUSSELBURGH until his son Willie Jnr joined him in the late 1870's. The stamp then became W. PARK & SON or Wm. PARK & SON.

Collectors will be able to find Park clubs at auctions and salerooms – they are also in "junk" shops around the country – but do beware of the "doctored" and refurbished implements which flaunt themselves as genuine; I have been offered them on more than one occasion, but the sharp stamping invariably gives them away.

Many W. Park clubs (stamped so, on the head) have Wm. Park & Son stamped on the shaft. This, of course, places the owner in a dilemma: what date does he put on it? I personally look upon it as a Park Senior head circa. 1870, reshafted probably some 15/20 years later when young Willie was with his father. Collectors should not worry unduly over this matter of the stamp on the shaft being different from that on the head, particularly on wood-headed clubs. Shafts, which were very slender from the middle of the 19th century, suffered terminal injury from hard hitting players and had to be replaced frequently, at the same time the club would probably be fitted with a new grip.

Park's iron heads came from various sources, including three of the local blacksmiths in Musselburgh. Some of the Park Senior heads will be of a slightly speckled metal, particularly his cleek and lofting irons. They are the treasures of the collectors. Should anyone be fortunate enough to find an iron punched with five "dots" on the blade, it was a club used by Willie Park Junior. He, too, made famous a wry-necked putter stamped Park Patent, the originals are greatly prized though they are not uncommon at the major auctions.

W. DUNN

Another famous name opened a clubmaking shop at Musselburgh in the 1870's – this was DUNN. Willie DUNN had been "keeper of the green" at Leith for some time, but as the clubs and societies moved out, so did he. Clubs marked W. DUNN are much sought after, so will not be cheap. A scare-headed wood is a very desirable addition to any collection. Irons were stamped in the same fashion as the woods.

Towards the end of the 19th century there were other established clubmakers at Musselburgh, making wood-headed clubs and shafting iron heads bought from St. Andrews. The names of W. Ballantyne, C. Davidson, R. Ferguson, T. Hood, P. Paxton and R. Neilson (the latter, being apprenticed to W. Park, was the last practising clubmaker at the links) all require a mention, but they had small businesses compared with the others.

To keep the record straight, I will return to Edinburgh for a moment to acknowledge two cleekmakers about whom I have very little information: the Scottish Golf Club Manufacturing Co., Albert Street, Edinburgh, Golf Club Manufacturers 1888, and Stirling & Gibson, Golf Cleek and Iron Makers, Jordan Lane, Edinburgh, advertising throughout 1889. J. P. Cochrane & Co. Ltd. was also established in the capital City.

later mark of BISHOP & HENDRY

HENDRY & BISHOP

Although I have earlier mentioned Bishop and Hendry of Leith, it is necessary to expand a little further on their workmanship. The Company originated as Bishop and Hendry, manufacturing saddlery metal fittings before immersing themselves with golf equipment. Changing their name to Hendry &

Bishop in 1911, they moved to West Port, Edinburgh and, turning out iron heads, used the cleek-marks of a Bishop's Mitre and later, a Cathedral. The Mitre Brand (blade unstamped) was supplied to many clubmakers, Sayers, Brodie and Park among them. Hendry & Bishop's "Cardinal" model clubs are widespread, many with the flanged sole became very popular.

BEN SAYERS
NORTH BERWICK
Old Mark

Travelling eastward from Edinburgh one can see the present day courses of Royal Musselburgh, Longniddry, Luffness, Gullane Nos. 1, 2 and 3 and Muirfield before arriving at North Berwick, where the one cleekmaker of East Lothian was established – namely, Ben Sayers. A diminutive man, tutor of nobility, princes and kings, golfer extraordinaire; a great competitor in championships and challenge matches; one wonders what he might have achieved had he been 6″ taller. Initially a ball-maker, Sayers' irons were made by Hendry & Bishop, Stewart, and others in Fife. In 1924 Ben Sayers Junior who had joined his father and was well established in the business, began forging iron-heads. Their first mark was a bird standing with its tail pointing to the ground . . . crow fashion. Later the bird ("Birdie" model) was much like a large wren, with the tail feathers up. Collectors can find both clubs as a nice matching pair.

BEN SAYERS
2nd Mark

It is rumoured that an iron foundry in North Berwick, owned by Bridges, turned out a few heads, probably by the employees for their own and their friends' use; this is, however, unsubstantiated.

So having looked at the majority of Scottish cleek and iron-head makers, we can now examine the prominent names with their cleek-marks, South of the Border. Let me pause for a moment or two in Sunderland; land of aluminium clubs – the most difficult implement to re-shaft ever made, due to the thinness of their sockets.

The Standard Golf Co. under the guidance of a Sir William Mills, first took out their patents in the late 1890's. All clubheads, cast in moulds, were of aluminium or aluminium and wood, each club, from driver to niblick, fashioned in a style comparable to the small wood-headed cleek of the 1900 era. Putters of every conceivable design came off the drawing boards, many of them becoming favourites of prominent professionals such as James Braid, Ted Ray and George Duncan. The early attraction of the clubs was the "feel" through the hands, of the core-wound ball striking aluminium as opposed to striking steel. Collectors can keep an eye open for aluminium heads with wood inserts, either in the face or in the back of the club. The company had no cleek-mark as such, but on the top of the head is the wording "Standard Golf Co. Sunderland". On the sole, particularly on putters, are the model details, and usually the weight and the "lie" of the club. Mills made left-handed clubs as well as right, but a "special" to look for is the two-faced implement which served the player well when confronted by an awkward stance.

To Birmingham next, where the name of Allday became synonymous with bronze and brass-headed putters. Most clubs were fitted with plain flat bladed heads – puttable with either side. Many were stamped with the name Mitchell – a store in Manchester – but Allday himself did not stamp them in any way. The clubs are difficult to identify and date; the hosel perhaps giving the best clue with deep, irregular chisel marks where the hickory shaft is inserted. The clubs were made from the late 1880's.

Blackheath Golf Co.
BY SPALDING

Travelling south-east we come to the famous Royal Blackheath Golf Club. It was inevitable that a company named Blackheath Golf Company be founded; the club is, without question, the oldest in England and a supplier and repairer had to be settled within the vicinity. The iron heads were stamped with a blacksmith's "tongs", but those heads were mostly forged by Spalding Brothers.

F. JOHNSON LTD
LONDON

In London, F. A. Johnson trading as F. A. Johnson Ltd., housed an adequate stock of assorted golf clubs; and while manufacturing woods, he acquired the experience and expertise of Hugh Logan (ex Gibson of Kinghorn) to produce irons. He endorsed his clubs with the cleek-mark of a "key", and under the watchful eye of Logan turned out a fair quantity of irons which had – to my eye as well as other clubmakers – the hall mark of Gibson in them. The company went into liquidation in 1910, thus leaving the collector an item which is rare rather than plentiful.

A Maltese Cross branded some woods, and all irons of F. H. Ayres of London. Their first irons came from Andersons, but around 1910 they began forging in their own foundry, and good models emanated from there. They made a particularly attractive putter "The Sandwich", which was long and shallow in the blade. The firm is reputed to have been founded early in the 19th century, catering for "sporting people"; it took them some time to latch on to the idea of making iron clubs!

CLAN
REGD
GOLF CO
LONDON

The Army and Navy Stores is in existence to this day, but in the last quarter of the 19th century the company was titled The Army and Navy Co-operative Society Ltd.; a wholesaler to the

Services. Golfing equipment had to be carried in their Sports Departments, and after selling golf balls and clubs made in Fife, they employed their own clubmakers.

One of Scotland's famous Open Champions, James Braid, served in the workshops, and it was there his fame as a golfer spread. His five Championship wins came while at Romford and when professional at Walton Heath. The two colleagues he worked with had their own special set of woods initialled after them: B.S.D. Braid, Smith and Davis. Some will say, Driver, Brassie and Spoon!

Collectors should have little difficulty finding a club, particularly an iron, and certainly a brass putter, with initials A. & N.C.S.L. stamped on the blade.

I realise I may have overlooked certain names as I have "travelled" the country, but as many of the cleek-marks are not direct from the manufacturer, but bear the mark of the professional, personalising them, I propose to collate and name them in a Second Division form. Those marks are the headache of the researcher; an acorn or an oak-tree could belong to the OKE family of professionals; it is fun finding out. It takes time.

W. OKE

BY F. H. AYRES

9. VIGILANCE IS THE KEY

WHILE describing cleek-marks of the South of England, there are one or two more prominent stampings which cannot be overlooked.

I show the "Shell" and "Pyramid" signs of J. B. Halley & Co. Ltd. of London; another mark was that of a double oval ring with the letters J.B.H. inside. There are not a great many of such irons turning up, so £3 or £4 can be well spent here. Incidentally a further stamp which I strongly suspect also belonged to J. B. Halley – after the turn of the century – is that of the letter "H" stylishly shown in a circle. I am unable to confirm its authenticity.

A "Coronet" was the cleek-mark on irons sold at one time by the Blackfriars Sports Company, clubs circa 1910. A nice mark. Lockwood Brown is another name that can be added to the collection. It was a sports store in Jermyn Street, London, that had models stamped with the entwined initials "LB". The heads were forged by Gibson of Kinghorn. A personalised stamp.

Jack White Golf Company is reputed to have made iron heads in his Oxford Street factory. The heads have his name on the blade, JACK WHITE, LONDON. Mr White was pro at Sunningdale for some 25 years . . . he won the Open Championship from there in 1904, with the score of 296, the first time the final total was below 300. As he was runner-up in the Open in 1899, 3rd in 1903 and 4th in 1900, I think his success was well merited.

The mark of Cann and Taylor (the "fliweel") shown earlier will be found on many irons; particularly irons made just around and after the turn of the century with J. H. Taylor's autograph on the blade. Taylor – one of the "Great Triumvirate" – won the Open Championship five times; the first Englishman to win the Open on English soil. His partnership with Cann – the clubmaker of the Company – flourished in East Sheen, Surrey, in the early 1900's, and on their success they opened a factory in the U.S.A., but this was relatively short-lived. Assembling a "set" of J. H. Taylor Autograph clubs can be an ideal pastime for the collector who has a single-minded interest. There is also TAYLOR'S MASHIE to be found, a deep bladed club for heavier lies.

J. B. HALLEY & CO. LTD.

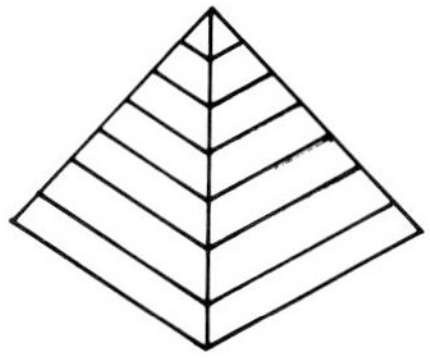

J. B. HALLEY & CO. LTD.

J. B. HALLEY & CO. LTD.

J. B. HALLEY

LOCKWOOD BROWN
LONDON

FLIWEEL
CANN & TAYLOR

JACK WHITE
LONDON

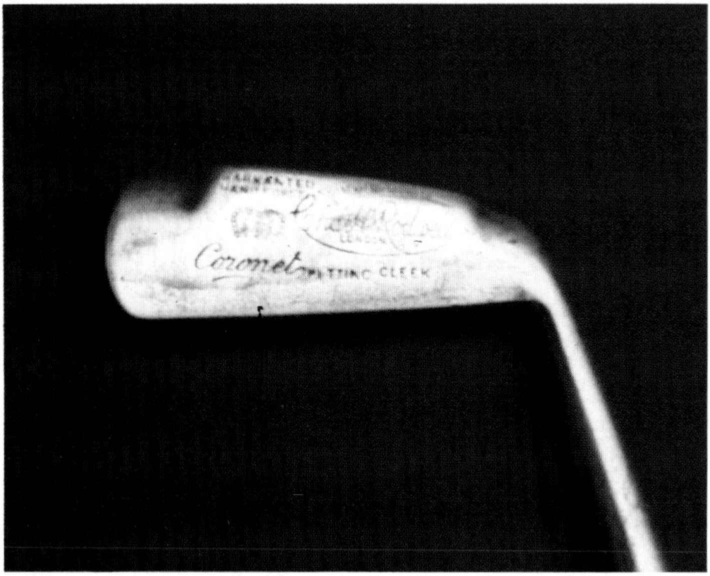

A putting cleek clearly stamped with the Coronet motif.

C G C

Castle Golf Co.

CASTLE GOLF CO.

C. GIBSON WESTWARD HO

Slazenger, a household name in the sporting world, had large premises in London just before 1900. They stamped their clubs not only with their own name, but gave model names to "sets". The "Boodie" clubs, are collectables, as are "St. Andrews" and "Fife" irons.

McGregor clubs were sold in London by the sports departments in the major stores. They were imported from the U.S.A. in the late 1890's and after 1900. It is understood they employed – in the U.S.A. – emigrants from Fife, and one can recognise the similarity of the shapes and models which St. Andrews, Anstruther and Kinghorn made famous. The cleek-mark of a clover leaf and a flower akin to a rose is indented on the blade of irons; occasionally both marks will appear on a club. A nicely defined EYE was the stamping used by Rollins & Parker.

J. Wisden, Cranborne Street, London, stocked many clubs of all models in their store. Stock was bought in from Forgan, Auchterlonie, Morris and Ben Sayers. It is noticeable that the Company invariably stamped its name on the hickory shaft.

The Castle Golf Company, London. S.E. symbolised its iron heads with two types of castle. It also used the design of the flag, the Union Jack, as a second mark.

Over on the South West Coast of England lies the famous links of Westward Ho! a true North Devon championship course. Its fame includes the name of Gibson; master clubmaker. Many clubs with perfect hickory can be acquired, fitted to iron heads

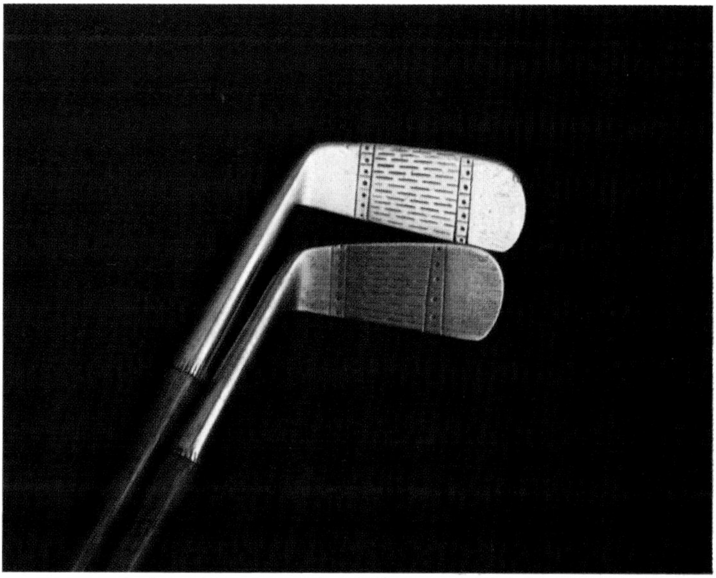

Face markings on putter and putting cleek.

mostly made by his name-sake Gibson of Kinghorn, C. Gibson was one of the early pros with a "personalised" stamping, that of a prancing horse, which may be varied in pose according to the smith who branded them. Certain clubs will depict the horse shown in level, "uphill" or "downhill" position.

In Birmingham, at Ashton Cross, iron and steel heads were being forged by Smethwick Golf Company in 1912; its name stamp appears on the club blade, but not any particular brand mark. Hemmings Golf Co. and Rollins & Parker both of Reddich were manufacturing iron heads about 1910.

BENETFINK
LONDON

BY ROLLINS & PARKER

Reminding readers at this time that I have been covering parts of Scotland and England, describing the cleek-marks on irons with which to build their collection, I have concentrated on a number of the major names and stamps which more readily come to hand. It leaves others for detailing, and many of renown are worth seeking, though there may be no symbol on the clubhead. However, I propose at this juncture to turn the head of the iron and write a few lines regarding the face of the club.

STANDARD GOLF CO
BIRMINGHAM

While giving circa 1895 as a "starting" date, please do not assume that *all* smooth faced clubs must therefore have been produced 5 years before 1900. It is known that smooth faced or unmarked irons were used with the newly invented rubber ball as late as 1908. I assume it was the older players with their favourite models who were responsible for such a situation; they obviously did not concern themselves too much with getting "grip" or

TRU FLIGHT

LEYLAND & BIRMINGHAM
RUBBER CO

"stop" on the golf ball. The early markings on the clubfaces were mainly punch marks, "dots" or identations: lines and grooves, whether straight, oval or circular, followed soon after.

Here again we can pause for a moment and ask ourselves the question "why did it take so long for golfers of the second-half of the 19th century to realise that marking on a clubface would improve the control of the ball"? Bear in mind the original feathery and gutta percha balls were smooth, so were erratic in flight. When the balls became hacked about and were eventually machine scored, they flew better. We might now think the clubface could have received similar treatment, lines or marks to match the ball . . . which would have produced the desired efffect of gripping the ball.

In relation to the ball marking, it was over 40 years later that the fashion of punch-marking of the club began.

As I said earlier, the patterns on the iron face were many and varied; Fairlie's anti-shank models were dotted overall, Gibson's Baxpin had crossed lines with dots, Nicoll had horizontal scores, Sayers pitchers had slanted scores, and Stewart had a 12 line face with a double perpendicular dotted design, most of the latter with unmarked toe and heel.

At the turn of the century many professionals had their clubs *deeply* grooved, seeking backspin when the ball was firmly punched out of the turf; however, they were soon caught up by the R. & A. when it was found the lines or dots were too deep, or the edges were rough or serrated, so a limit to the depth and width was laid down, and is in fashion to the present day.

Having said a word or two about the faces of the irons, I will once again return to the matter of the markings on the side which never sees the ball; I can continue to show those cleek-marks which were widespread, along with those that were "local". In using that latter word I refer to personalised stamps; clubs made by a manufacturer for the professional or sports store who wished to have their own brand or model.

Recently I mentioned Scott of Elie (Fife) with three stamps, the lion, lion and crown, and finally, a star added. This trio of marks is shown to enable the new collector to recognise his irons, which were usually supplied by the Anderson factories in the county.

Sherlock, Ray and Turner, three prominent pros just after the 1900's began, formed a mini co-operative, enabling themselves to buy finished clubs cheaply. Their stamp a circle with the surname initials within. Turner designed clubs which he named

Sherlock, Ray & Turner

WELL MADE

A. PATRICK, LEVEN

GRAMPIAN RANGE
for Turner by W. Gibson

the Grampian range, at present I am unable to tell who forged the iron heads. I have been told they were by W. Gibson & Co. Ltd.

Along with Nicoll, another well-known clubmaking family sited in Leven was that of Patrick. This firm was established before Nicoll, but concentrated on wood-heated clubs. The cleek-mark which varies greatly on their irons, is that of a person walking through a "horseshoe", or what I think was originally a design of a lady walking through the archway of an ancient building. As she was carrying a fairly large load of her head I suspect she was on her way to the links with washing where, history tells us, the locals were at liberty to use the ground (sand, "bent" grass and gorse) as a "drying green". Patrick's metal stamps were obtained from different sources. Accepting the family were one of the oldest clubmakers in Fife, it is more than likely that they obtained their iron heads from either Anderson or Stewart of St. Andrews.

Goudie and Christie, two names stamped on smooth faced irons and lofters of circa 1890, may occasionally be found, but from 1910 onwards J. T. Goudie & Co., who were manufacturing woods in Miller Street, Glasgow, also sold irons supplied by Winton of Montrose. A capital G in a circle would appear to be their identification.

Two Glasgow Golf Co. marks are that of a Thistle, something similar to the McEwan stamp, though with the leaves more widely spaced. The second mark, a square, with GLASGOW GOLF CO. within, but bisected by the name PIRIE. Alex. M. Pirie took over the company after the First World War, but they eventually dropped the marks, and stamped the blade A.M.PIRIE.

A. M. PIRIE

Still in Glasgow, the name of Lumley was prominent; many of its irons are to be found, including attractive junior clubs (so stamped), their identification being that of crossed sabres, which may have the "point" upwards or downwards. Frequently a letter of the alphabet – H – may be idented between the sabre blades – a model by Halley.

LUMLEY GLASGOW

By now you have the details of some 80 stamps or "cleek-marks". I hope that the foundations or framework of a collection has begun, and that you are able to identify the manufacturers from the symbols shown. Do bear in mind there will be slight variations in some of the designs, because it was not only the iron-head makers who went out of business, but the stamp makers too. Spare a thought for those craftsmen when you look at the intricacies of some of the cleek-marks. Artists in their own right they had to be, for whenever a new or replacement stamp was ordered, the original had, after being beaten on hundreds of iron heads, lost its sharpness, and clarity. The "Hand of Friendship", symbol of Nicoll of Leven, is an example of such an occurrence, the original position of the thumb altered on the new hand . . . but it made little or no difference to the company, it was still the well renowned hand.

P. G. Allday & Co Ltd Birmingham

Recently discovered stampings include "The Northwood" (by P. G. Allday & Co. Ltd.) which will be seen on aluminium headed putters, and the "Comet" symbol which is a secondary mark of Craigie of Montrose (who had a rifle on most of his iron blades). I suspect Craigie made a complete set with the "Comet" stamp, as I have seen wooden-headed clubs similarly marked.

Craigie of Montrose

10. SEARCHING FOR THE PERFECT CLUB

WHILE writing on the subject of "Collecting", I have often thought that the humble aspirants of yesteryear, smitten by the Royal and Ancient game, could also deserve the accolades afforded and bestowed upon the giants of the links of today.

This is prompted by the investigation and researching which confirm the difficulties and "hazards" of the game; whether it involved the conditions of the terrain, or the clubs and balls which were used throughout the past century and a half. It was a tortuous pastime indeed. The problems of scoring a fair total with the implements of the time, on fairways and greens which were incondite and unkempt, must have sorely tried the patience of the majority of players, and it would be no surprise to me if the greater percentage of participants vowed, at some time or other, "never to play the game again"!

Are we not the same today? Even though we have everything necessary to aid us to the peak of perfection – or at least I think we have – the occasional bad round, or even a few disastrous holes, bring on that feeling of despondency and despair, which tempts us to write the obituary of our golf bag and its contents.

Fortunately, however, the game is played in most countries of the civilised world – as are many other sports and pastimes – but as golf has no index, because of its being so wholly individualistic, someone somewhere is trying to master it. It is "man's" ideal looking for the state of perfection which, in the ultimate, can never be reached.

Thanks be, therefore, to a lesser number who, with play-clubs and spoons, cleeks, lofters, mashies, track-irons and putters, persisted in firstly knocking about the links a leather ball stuffed with a top-hatful of feathers; followed by a "revolutionary" ball, the "gutty", and superseded by a Haskell ball, kept the game alive, fanning the embers until it flamed throughout our Islands; and because we are essentially a benevolent people we eventually passed it to our friends across the seas.

I have already written, the oldest known clubs and balls were used on tracts of land which, instead of being spelt "course", may well have been coarse. Certainly the implements could not strike the ball any great distance, because their make-up was crude and the links looked uncared for. The garb of the players – particularly the men – was completely ill-suited for a rhythmic swing; a collar and tie or cravat was usually worn, and pictures of the early professionals show a buttoned up jacket, fairly well tailored, except where the large left-hand pocket housed five or six golf balls, obviously to replace those which shattered.

Progress rolled on however and if we skip a few decades and move to the beginning of the 1900's, men, machines and implements were becoming sufficiently sophisticated to be altering the game.

It is in this context that I relate the comparisons of golfers of then and now. Who will argue against Andrew Kirkaldy's "best holes" score at St. Andrews of 2,2,3,3,2,3,3,2,1 = 21 out, 2,1,2,3,4,2,3,3,2 = 22 in, totalling 43 as being GREAT; bearing in mind the difficulties of which I have written during his years from 1870 as a boy, to manhood in the late 1920's? Who cannot equate Henry Cotton's 65 of the 1934 Open Championship with similar scores of today? (Whereupon a Dunlop ball was born.) He also had a 62 on Brockenhurst Manor, 63 at Ashridge and 64 at Wentworth West. Give Henry today's facilities and he would equal the best.

So, while supersonic aircraft and rockets to the moon have been *invented*, golf has *progressed* fortunately leaving for us, numerous objects of interest, curiosity and wonder, which we, at long last, are pouncing upon as golf antiques and collectables.

Having looked at the comparisons of man against the changes of facilities, let me return again to the iron clubs with which I have dealt before. Firstly, I will, however, say a few words about *model* marks or names on the iron blade. In point of fact I am quite unable to do justice to this matter, because certain manufacturers – the larger ones – made dozens of models over a period of time, and it would be a mammoth task in itself to collate them. Therefore let me quote the more popular names that turn up.

Very early clubs did not have model names; it was around the turn of the century that, alongside the manufacturer's symbol, the design details were stamped, and this went on continually up to the Second World War. I am aware it also followed 1945.

I feel sure most collectors have found the "Genii" model by H. Logan of Gibson of Kinghorn, probably also stamped Maxwell, "The socket with the holes in it". Many of these irons are available as Gibson's production was enormous.

Having mentioned a Fife iron-head maker, others in the same

county such as D. Anderson & Son with their "Glory", "Ellice" and "Sovereign" models; Forgan with the "Celtic", "Crown" and "Scotia". In Leven, G. Nicoll was noted for the "Gem" putter along with the old "Zenith" irons. Alex Patrick produced the fine "Perfector" model around 1910. Condie of St. Andrews sold a "Triumph" putter, as did Anderson & Son, and it is possible the clubs came from one source. "The Prince" was a Bishop and Gourlay product; "The Scuffler" and "Varsity" by Spence & Gourlay. "The Spieler" and "The Cert", Winton of Montrose. Cochrane modelled "The Dedli", while Spalding stamped many clubs with "Gold Medal", because they did so well in the competitions which were open to manufacturers from 1906 onward. Spalding irons with the name DYSART, FIFE, are rarer than their other models, so might be worth a £1 more if you feel so inclined.

I should also mention that certain head makers stamped the name of the model on the sole of the iron, instead of the reverse of the blade. It is not the first time that while I have inspected the details of the manufacturer in the expected place, I have discovered – usually under rust and grime – additional wording, which is the model, on the *sole*. Pitching clubs and putters are more prone to this than others, so inspect the blade closely, perhaps you will find the word "Chipper", "Baxpin", "Stopum" or "Bogee" on the area of the club which sits on the ground. It will not, however, put any greater value on the implement.

Returning to the model details alongside the "cleek-mark", I must say there are many of each for investigation. Owing to duplication, at least three manufacturers stamped clubs either "Accurate" or "The Accurate". Anderson obviously had not registered the arrow symbol for the firm, so there was nothing to hinder others depicting the "missile" which was indicative of accuracy. Greater care is taken now to inform the patents office.

There were numerous model names given to wood headed clubs too. In fact most top-line clubmakers – particularly those professionals who were in shops of their own, or attached to Golf Clubs – *did* have a "special" of their own design.

Names that spring to mind, or have been recorded, were James Bradbeer with his "Sure to Win" logo. F. Hockins with brass ferrules (instead of whipping or twine) on the socket, as "The Everlasting". Robert Bell Martin stamped his round sole wood putter with "R.B.M. model". A. J. Rowe, famous (the advert claims) for his "Toby" brassie-spoon, and last but not least, J. H. Taylor's "Confidus" woods, which were no doubt

F. H. AYRES

G. NICOLL

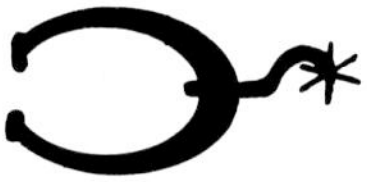
A. PATRICK OF LEVEN

GLASGOW GOLF CO.

completed by Cann of the Cann & Taylor partnership.

So that the continuity of "mark" collecting does not suddenly cease, I detail further samples for the enthusiast. Martin and Kirkaldy are names that are to be found on many iron heads. A plain "hand-written" stamp in very fine writing. The "Kirkaldy" Autograph is to be found too. They did not make the heads themselves but bought them in from Forgan and Tom Stewart of St. Andrews. You have seen the B. & S. A. mark of Brodie & Son, Anstruther; there was also another cleek or iron maker in the same town with the name Brodie & Co. with the initial within a circle. Established in Glasgow in the late 1880's was Brodie Breeze & Co., I suspect their mark around 1910 was that of a bee. They were also in Anstruther in 1913.

A second mark of F. H. AYRES keeps cropping up, that of a Buffalo, a later model, after the First World War; as was G. Nicoll's "Punch" model. A further addition to the Glasgow Golf Company's symbols is that of a Stag's head, (head and antlers only), not to be confused with the leaping Stage of St. Andrews Golf Company. Alex Patrick of Leven, Fife, used a unique form of spur as a secondary mark prior to 1910. If you are collecting "marks" only, I trust they will soon come to hand.

Now for a brief look at the "handle" end of the club – the "grip".

Those who already have in their possession some of the older relics of the mid and second half of the 19th century, will undoubtedly have noticed the type of packing below the thickened grips of their clubs. The materials often varied dependent upon the clubmaker, but they mostly came under the name of "listing" or "rind". Fabrics such as flannel, serge, linen and thick woollen cloth were all put to good purpose and while layering one piece over another, using "tacky" pitch as a "non slip" agent, a correct taper was obtained by regulating the length of material used. From around 1910 the "packing" was frequently covered by a layer of double sided adhesive tape – a black sticky fabric roll common to the electrical trade – this had an ideal surface for the leather on which to grip.

Early grips were of sheepskin – Philp used many of them with the "prepared" or smooth side out – tanned cowhide and horsehide, the former having the nap side out, forming a suede of "coarser" feel. Various hides were used; some being perforated as a simulated pigskin; others with the edges chamfered to give ease to the fitting of the leather grips, which were in vogue in the 1900's. Names prominent in the preparation of skins and grips were Balmforth Ltd. (Yorks), Cameron & Son (Fife) later famed for their "Kinghorn Tacky Grip", Fulford Grip Co. (Yorks) and Hewitt & Sons (Edinburgh) who tried pigskin for some time, but reverted to calfskin.

Early in the 20th century, along with leather, came the Rubber grips, also "American Cloth" which appeared to be a rubber solution covering thick linen.

Rubber grips were thicker and narrower than leather – consequently they were much longer – and the tighter the clubmaker wound them round the "handle", the more pronounced became the ridges which improved the hand security of the player. They were not popular in wet weather however – gloves were not too fashionable at that time – and in very hot weather they became soft and sticky, making them altogether too precarious to hold. Nevertheless great names manufactured them, including The India Rubber, Gutta Percha and Telegraph Works Co. Ltd. (a marvellous heading for envelopes!). The Leyland & Birmingham Rubber Co., The North British Rubber Co. Ltd. and The Avon Rubber Co. Ltd.

The "American Cloth" grip was a cheaper product put on many inexpensive clubs, or replacements for those who played little golf. Their lifetime in the 1920's-30's was relatively brief.

So it can be seen that from the 1880's, the alterations to the golf club grip have been minimal, only the fabric succumbing to change. From tanned leather, rubber, and rubber-compound (the U.S.A. mixture) back to leather which was used on most good clubs in the period I am covering up to the early 1920's.

I often wonder when I see the present "rubberised" slip-on tube-like grips of today, how long we shall wait for a quality leather to re-adorn a golf club. Not long perhaps. Leather grips were amenable to treatment – to preserve, clean and bring them back to a usable state by wiping them with a mixture of methylated spirit and castor oil – or is there a more suitable material or substance to make up the ideal grip? I venture to suggest that the greater percentage of clubmakers who worked on hickory shafts would agree that leather has no peer.

It is of interest that the grips (including packing) of the first half of the 20th century were much lighter in weight than those of today; despite the fact that the early structure was of four or five pieces of material, compared with one.

I hope that many newcomers to the hobby have met with success, particularly acquiring clubs at prices which create an investment. Personally, I am amazed at the number of old and antique implements still being discovered. Major auction houses offer "tenon-joint", "one-piece", crossheads and well-named spliced woods; while track-irons, rut-niblicks and curious putters are still being found in out-houses, attics and cellars.

11. HOW TO LOOK AFTER YOUR CLUBS

HAVING dealt with the more common cleek-marks and knowing that collectors are ferreting out old clubs from all manner of places, the time has come to pass on information regarding the treatment and care of these implements, particularly the metal-headed clubs.

Readers will have noted that irons of my own collection are, in some cases, completely rusty; others range from mottled brown to shiny, (none is highly polished or "buffed", the flash bulb of a camera shot is responsible for the extra brightness on certain pictures).

I readily acknowledge that my way is not necessarily correct in every respect, but over the years in which I have been involved in clubmaking, particularly hickory shafted irons, etc., I find my fellow collectors with experience differ little in their methods, to mine.

Collectors who have decided to burnish their iron clubs, please carry on. I have admired small displays which are very attractive to the eye, so I do not condemn; we are still in a fraternity amassing the implements of the game, it is our hobby.

The very ancient clubs, used before the middle of the 19th century – clubs which came face to face with the feathery ball – are likely to be very dry and rusty, the majority turning up now will possibly be *thick* with rust, and it is here I suggest you find someone with experience to decide whether it is right to remove the rust or not. In my view, if it is wholly crusted leave it alone and save your energy, the chances of finding a mark or a name are slight. You may make your own decision as to removing the rust from the *back* of the blade, but the implement will look unsightly if only partly cleaned; it will make it look more like a curio.

Everyone at some time or other has found and had to remove rust from a particular object, so they will have an idea of its behaviour . . . rust always seems to return after cleaning; and even following a light smearing of oil the atmospheric dust will coat it with "fur". Iron, when old and dry – and *kept very dry* – will last decades; it seems to have grown impervious to further pollution around it, so here is where I say "leave well alone". I know you will soon find out what type of club you possess . . . a cleek, lofter, track iron, etc., so have it dated approximately, identified if possible and be proud to possess it as it stands.

Less rusty irons are not such a problem. After 1850 the smooth faced clubs sometimes had stampings, mainly those made for or by Carrick, Cossar, Gray and Wilson, etc. so those implements deserve careful treatment and investigation. My personal collection of "tools" for cleaning an iron head are scant indeed. Two double-sided "spongy" emery blocks; one rough and smooth, the other smooth and fine. (Bought from any ironmonger.) Two pads of wire wool again – smooth and fine – and a small handled wire brush – suitable for cleaning suede shoes – to clear out the stampings. A ¾″ wide roll of plastic adhesive tape – for wrapping around the wood shaft where it enters the hosel – a handful of absorbent rags, and a small quantity of water. (Remember the Army phrase "spit and polish" – water is a boon to me in club-cleaning.)

Curiosity compels me to attack the back of the iron blade first, mainly to certify its breed. If it is particularly rusty, I wet the end of the coarser wire wool, or the emery block, and rub to and fro, heel to toe, wiping the blade regularly with a rag, drying, then wetting it until most of the heavier rust has gone. I finish it off with a fine wool or smooth emery pad. During this process, dampness is in the name or "cleek stamp", so a careful polishing with the fine brush – I think it is brass wire – should move out much of the rust gathered there and, with luck, the details become apparent.

Frequently old clubs have had the name, etc. completely erased; caddies – and owners – have cared for them so well that the manufacturer's work has been "ground" away and only guesswork is left to identify the make.

Regarding the cleaning of the remainder of the head, the task is straightforward. I remove the rust from the face, the top and bottom of the blade in exactly the same fashion as the back, and rub the toe and heel of the club as if wiping a ball.

Finally, the socket or hosel. I tightly wrap adhesive tape exactly at the joint with the shaft. Holding the soft pads, which are supple enough to wrap around the socket, I place the end of the shaft on the ground then rotate the club with my free hand on the toe of the blade. Using this method carefully, I prevent the shaft from being marked, but do get a required finish to the iron socket. I do not use liquid or paste rust remover, probably because I have not found one which is any more effective than the method used by caddies over the past two centuries; nor have I had the inclination to use a "buffing" machine which is electrically powered, and can burnished a club in minutes. I have detailed *my* method because it has served me well over many years and I don't suppose I'll change now!

Earlier I mentioned the matter of rust returning to newly cleaned heads. By experience I have found that within a matter of days the iron has frequently become brown again, which is a reaction to the warmth created on the surface of the metal, by the cold coming through the core. In such instances I clean the rust off lightly, rub it with metal polish and allow it to stand unpolished for a few days. By keeping the clubhead very dry, cleaning becomes a lesser chore. In conclusion: if you do desire, the iron head may be brushed over with a clear varnish to prevent discolouration; I have seen clubs in some collections finished in this way and they look quite satisfactory.

12. SHAFTS IN OLD CLUBS

IN THIS chapter I would like to spend a little time discussing the construction of the old iron clubs with particular reference to choosing and fitting the shaft.

You will see there are two *basic* designs of socket and most irons fall into these categories. In fact the "through socket" is pretty scarce, but every collector buys as many as he or she can afford – even for swaps.

The designs have been drawn as No. 1 and No. 2 and are self explanatory. From the clubmaker's point of view the through shafts – i.e. through hosel, the wood showing in the sole – were the simpler to make, and in fact I never saw anything wrong in this design providing there was sufficient weight in the bottom of the iron blade. The shafts did not break any more frequently than

Exploded view of the standard fitting of a wood shafted iron.

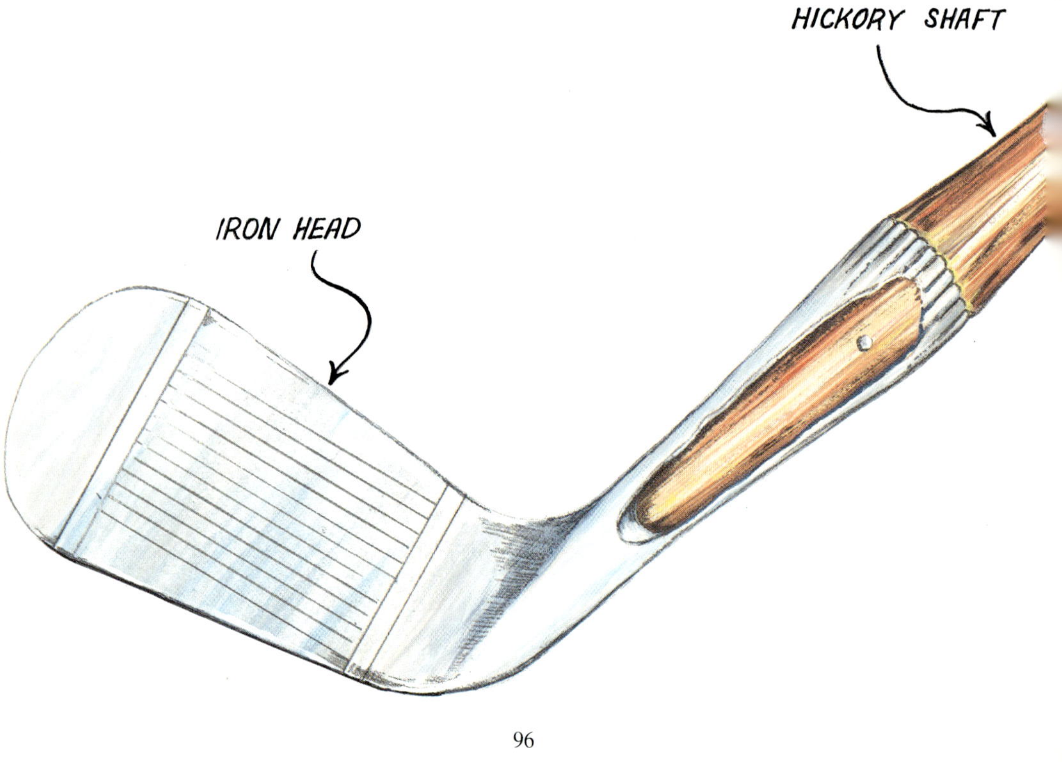

those of the fitted shaft, and indeed were driven in tightly without any "play" or "rock". Dampness affected them little.

"In days of yore" – from the beginning of the 19th century – we know that many types of tree and shrub were tried to find the best wood for shafts. For irons, particularly the heavily weighted track and sand irons, greenheart when well seasoned was robust and, because of its thickness, stood up better than lancewood or ash.

Lancewood, a grainless looking wood, could make a beautifully finished implement, but ash was the most suitable until the foreign hickory came in. Hickory in a variety of forms, white, red, ringed and plain, became the ideal shaft for woods and irons, more so that latter, as the poorer quality woods could be used for putters and chippers, etc.

Just a word about hickory, which is a distinctively grained wood, collectors will find it in varying degrees of hue. There are two reasons for this; one caused by the "colouring" of the shaft by clubmakers; the other due to the area where the timber was grown and the part of the tree from which it was cut. With the older clubmakers – and I was very fortunate to be trained by one

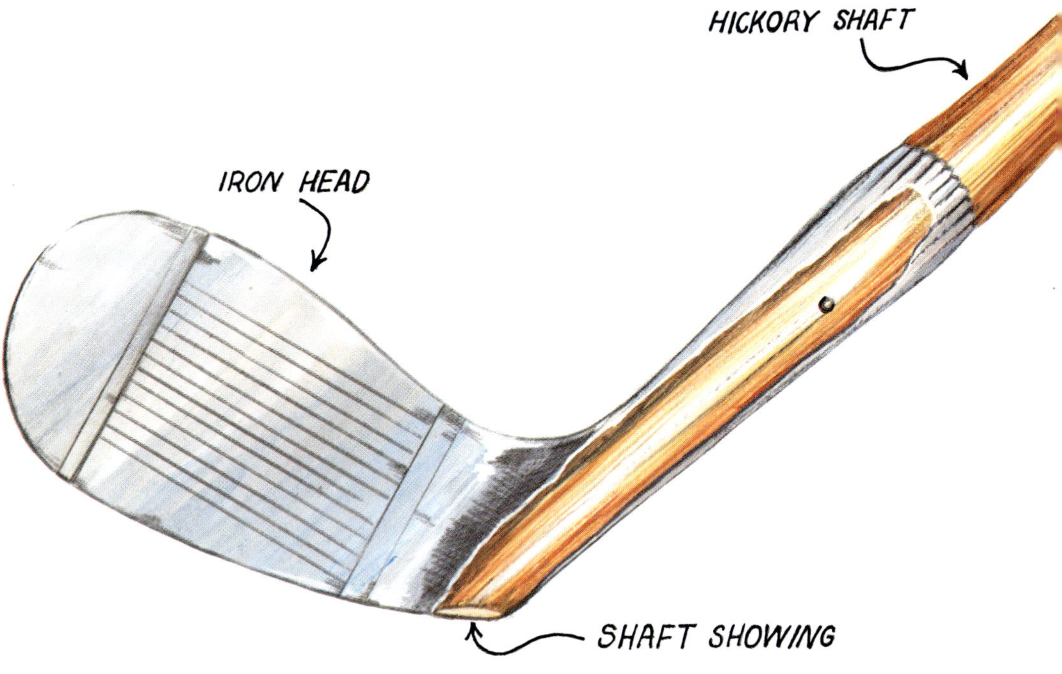

An iron (mashie niblick) with the shaft through to the sole.

– there was much inspection and selection given to the wood, particularly the shaft, before it was fitted. In the present day of reproduction clubs – mainly putters – I frequently see hickory shafts fitted incorrectly, even back to front, which in time may give trouble.

Perhaps at this time readers will not object to my explaining or describing the fitting of a hickory shaft into an iron club; a few collectors attempt it, but I think it always advisable to get it done by someone experienced, someone who has been in the club-making trade. I will not go back to the "unturned" wood (rods of hickory about ¾″ square), but will start with the prepared shaft i.e. the shaft slightly tapered to the socket end, and a flanged tongue roughly shaped for entry to the hosel. (Sketch A.) In

COMPLETE SHAFT STRAIGHT GRAINED HICKORY
A

B STRAIGHT GRAIN

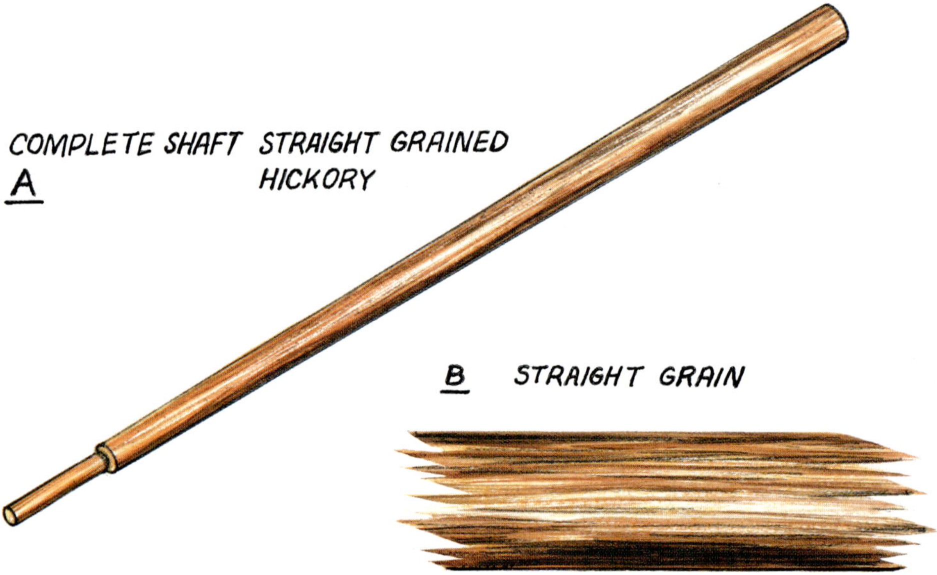

C 'ROSE' OR 'V' GRAIN

choosing a shaft for the longer iron, one selects the straightest grained wood, it will not bend so readily. (Sketch B.)

If you look closely at various shafts, you may notice that certain clubs have a grain mark, which appears under the pseudonym of "the rose" south of the border, but "V grain" where I was brought up in Scotland. These grain marks *tapering pointedly* in the shaft, may be seen distinctly on the back of the hickory; (Sketch C.) and this is where I explained there was a back and front to the shaft. While the "rose" or "V grain" is to the rear, the shaft will bend with the curve as in the form of a long-bow, which is the safer way of the bend. In fitting the new shaft to an iron head, the tongue was filed until it fitted tightly – by hand, the shaft was twisted around in the socket to enable the clubmaker to see the marks where the wood was ill-fitting. The shaft was then driven in to the socket until the two met up completely. The hole was then drilled through the socket to take the rivet which held the two together. This was quite a skilled job; it is not easy to bore through wood to meet the hole in the opposite side of the socket, so it was drilled part way from both sides. The danger here, however, was that if the bore didn't meet horizontally, when a rivet was inserted it could pull or push the head from its position on the shaft. If this occurred it sometimes meant an alteration to the flange of the shaft. In finishing the operation, by hammering down the rivet end until the "burr" was nearly flat, much smooth filing and buffing of the hosel had to be done to make the connection invisible, sufficient to match the polished head when necessary. With the iron head fitted, the "planeing", scraping and sandpapering of the shaft had to be done with care. One started at the socket with a medium file to bring the shaft down to a size similar to the hosel. Then with a hand plane – and here is where a fashion emanated from W. Park's premises – holding the clubhead, rotating the shaft all the time, the shaft was shaved while it lay in a grooved "rest", angled upward about 50°. This meant the plane "hit" the lower end of the shaft which is the slender end, and by the time the plane was pushed to the top, the pressure was lighter, thus creating a required taper. So the rough work was done.

To shape and style the shaft, the use of a steel "scraper" – a couple of grades of sandpaper – medium and smooth – gave it the finish, feel and "whip" the clubmaker required, even while the grip was unfitted.

Now should you wish to know the secrets of shaft colouring and finishing during bygone days, let me reveal the "processes" of the Lothian clubmakers. The smells of wood, oil, cellulose and varnish seemed to be pleasing to everyone, customers regularly asking to come into the workshops to see what was going on. Somewhere to the rear of the workbenches stood two tall canisters, one with iron filings and spirals of iron and steel off-cuts soaking in vinegar, producing a rusty coloured stain which rubbed on the shaft with a handful of wood shavings. This liquid not only coloured the wood as required, but raised the grain of the shaft, so a second sandpapering job had to be done.

The second canister held a concoction of oil, pitch, (kept soft by the oil) and a small quantity of methylated spirit. This messy substance was smeared on to the shaft with a makeshift "tool" (thick rag, wrapped around a piece of old hickory, which rested in the container), then a handful of wood shavings cleaned the lot off leaving a nicely darkened grain, ready for a cloth to smooth off the shaft. At this time it was left to dry out in preparation for its first varnish polish.

The initial coat of polish was put on by a wad of cotton wool wrapped in fine cotton cloth lightly dipped in Shellac with a spot of linseed oil. The pad was then rubbed from the socket to within 6″/8″ of the top of the shaft (the portion under the grip) giving it a smooth base before its final polish, which was completed after the leather "grip" had been fitted.

So, hopefully, you can visualise the fitting of a hickory shaft into an iron head. It was/is hard work if done in the old fashioned way, but electric machinery has transformed the whole operation now, and the real craftsmanship has gone. Nevertheless, a correctly balanced hickory shafted iron, made to suit the player, will prove for some time as effective as most steel shafted irons.

13. SHAFTS IN OLD CLUBS (Woods)

EARLIER, I divulged some of the methods, standard and otherwise, in which wooden shafts were fitted into *iron* heads; I now turn attention to the composition of the *wooden* headed implements which, in many instances, created more problems than the metal.

We who are interested in collecting, are aware of the alteration in design of wood heads of the mid 1800's to those of the 1920's. Initially long and tapered – shallow in the face; then shorter in the head; followed by a round to pear-shaped design, deeper in the face; which has not dramatically altered much in the past 50 years.

The socket of the "woods" (Drivers, Brassies, Baffies, Spoons, etc.) however went through three distinct changes which, perhaps more for the clubmakers than the players, revolutionised the game. (I refrain from including the "special" fitments of "tenon joint", "V" joints, "one piece" and other woods, as I wish to concentrate on the conventional clubs only).

The earliest woods had long tapering sockets which in effect were known as the "scared" or spliced headed clubs. The splice which was angled from the base of the socket, leaving thickness, was affixed to a contra-angled shaft which eventually matched the taper of the head.

Looking firstly at the shaft, a lengthy piece of (possibly) ash or (more likely from around 1860) straight-grained hickory, it was a relatively simple matter of planeing and filing a flat side to a point: not a needle point, a flat point! Fashioning the angle of taper on the *head* socket was the more difficult part of the operation; it had to "sit" or fit flush against the shaft without rocking in any way. The two pieces of wood – head and shaft – also had to marry up so that the club head sat on the ground without giving the appearance of being "toed-in" or hooked: nor dare it be "open-faced", which would encourage a slice.

When the clubmaker had satisfied himself that the shaft and head splice were correctly suited, he invariably checked the final fitment by temporarily binding the two pieces together with string. This added test was desirable prior to the finality of glueing. (A fish-glue up to the late 1920's which was distinctly more pungent than aromatic!)

The manufacture of spliced clubs direct from the bench fortunately had a tolerance; the craftsman had the opportunity to file and alter the sole of the club slightly so that it "sat" correctly. Not so the club which was being re-shafted or reset, the fitting of the two *had* to be level and flush together.

Incidentally, there is a rather unusual feature about spliced woods insomuch that when the "whipping" or twine was wound around the joint, a "tongue" of about 3/8" of shaft was seen on the socket of the head. This, if nothing else, is a great boon to collectors, it confirms the club is "scare-headed".

Splied heads, as far as we know, fashioned for over two centuries, continued to be made into the early 1900's, and though the clubhead had changed shape, players used them up to the First World War.

Following the "spliced" model, the socket club arrived, wherein the shaft entered the shorter neck of the head for 2" or 2¼". the "through socket" became popular too; the hole being drilled to enable the end of the shaft to emerge through the sole of the club.

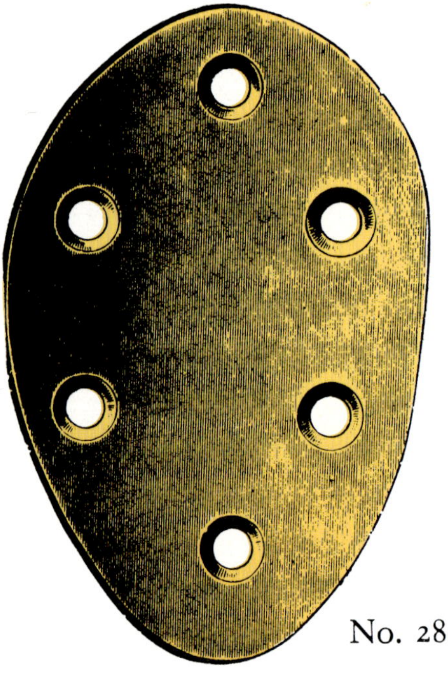

No. 2808 **20**/-

DRAWN ACTUAL SIZE.

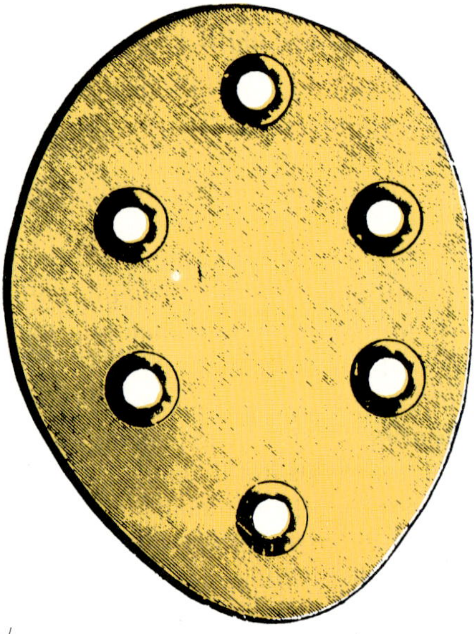

No. 2809 **19**/-

Providing the socket of the head was thick enough when the rough block was shaped, it was a simpler and quicker method of drilling the bore for the shaft. This became the standard fitment with hickory and with steel shafts.

While woods up to the first half of the 19th century were mainly fitted with horn in the base of the clubface, a later innovation was the addition of a "plate", mainly brass, being used as a protection to the club sole. The designs and shapes were many and varied, and in certain instances they give clues to the periods in which the clubmakers manufactured their models.

At this point I wish to thank P. A. Allday & Co. Ltd. of Birmingham, for their kindness in forwarding me a copy of a 1905 catalogue when they were – from 1895 – supplying brass and gun-metal heads (including juvenile), and brass "plates" for the soles of wood headed clubs. I feel sure there will be no objection if I mention that the "plates" were being sold at prices ranging from 12/6d. to 20/- per gross; and for quantity buying, were discounted by up to 15%.

In the late 1800's the brass plate was fitted to the bulger heads; and to the Brassies, Spoons and Baffies at the turn of the century. Initially, the rounded plate covered the sole completely, but

No. 2800 **20**/-

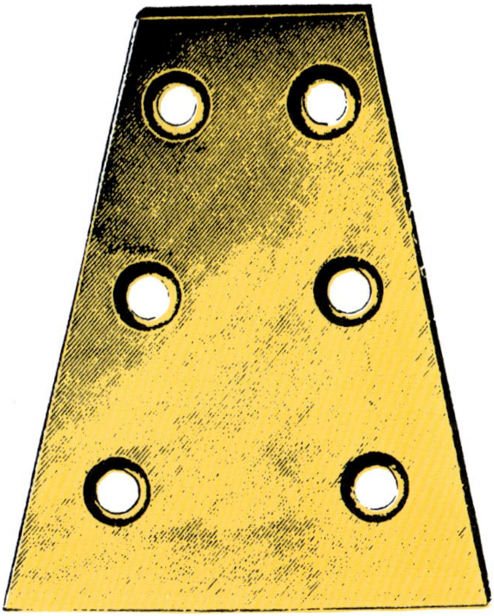

No. 2906 **18**/-

while the clubmakers were producing varying models of clubs, Allday & Co. also provided a wide range of sole plates to choose from.

In the early 1900's the plates changed shape, not only to enhance the look of the club, but to avoid the head being over-weighted by brass. Of course one factor in the clubmakers favour was that whenever a club required extra weight, it could be put under the plate by drilling a hole in the wood and filling it with molten lead.

A number of old woods may be found fitted with Centre Wedge Weights in place of the lead in the back of the clubhead. They were made in brass and aluminium and put a fine finish to the clubs.

So, having mentioned that the shaft and head fittings were glued on to, or into, the socket, then finally bound tightly with pitched twine – "whipping" to many – which was rubbed under pressure with "heel-ball" this brief synopsis of shafting a wood club is concluded. I trust it has given a little insight into "the other side of golf"! No doubt man – and machine – will continue to produce models and methods to simplify the popularity of the sport; and, alas, a club made from wood will only be a part of history.

No. 2915 **14**/-

No. 2907 **15**/-

14. FAKES AND FORGERIES

REGRETTABLY, a number of unscrupulous craftsmen are now turning their attention to implements of the Royal and Ancient game. Both wooden and iron headed clubs are being cleverly tampered with by skilled hands that will turn an ordinary cheap item into a so called valuable antique.

With the vast number of clubs made in days gone by, it is not too difficult to acquire something which will respond to alteration; nor is it beyond the capabilities of those able to handle tools to convert a fascimile into a relic. The experienced collector generally spots a fake by the treatment – cleaning, polishing, stamping and refurbishing – it has received, so alas it is the inexperienced and the unwary who become the victims. Can this be avoided? Unfortunately I fear not altogether, but a number of safeguards can be taken to prevent the new collector acquiring "copies". Firstly, if one is after a "prize possession", either have it authenticated, or purchase it from a reliable source. Obtain a receipt or guarantee if possible and there is no shame in saying you have bought it in good faith. Inspect every detail of a club carefully, particularly wood shafted irons, to see if they have been re-shafted or have insecure heads. The very old chamois grips – usually tan in colour – will be roughened and marked, and are helpful in confirming a club's age and value. The whipping or twine on the grip will help too, it can "date" a club at times; it *should* look old. Also inspect the grip end of a wooden shaft, it will be dark and smooth. Iron heads that are prone to alteration are numerous. Rut niblicks can be "ground down" on the top and toe of the blade; inspect the toe particularly, it should be pitted and indented by the flint and stone which lay in hoof marks and wheel tracks, similar to the dents and scratches on the sole.

Many track irons and rut niblicks – there is a difference between the two – which have been smoothed and sandpapered down, removing all detail from the back of the blade, may have been restamped, e.g. if not with the name of Carrick, by his small rough cross. Such a "cross" should looked aged, in keeping with the irregular cold chisel marks at the top of a long socket.

Cleeks are susceptible to blade narrowing, and old makers

who used block letters for stamping their names – W. PARK, DUNN, McEWAN, T. MORRIS, HUTCHISON and others – are at the mercy of the forger. In some cases certain acids will prove the "newness" of a recent stamping; equally, other acids will "eat" the iron and cause, along with rust, a head to look older than it is. (I have seen this on putter heads!) Replica clubs, too, are fair game for the swindler. Already I have been shown a long-headed spliced McEwan driver which was refitted with an old shaft, and with the head rescraped, battered about, restained and polished it was offered as an "oldie". Whoever spent their time on it had done a good job, but the horn in the leading edge of the sole had not been worn by time and use, so it was refused.

SCOTT OF ELIE

MONOPLANE

A number of putters now being reproduced, which have a name in coloured transfer form, are being "doctored" too. Watch out for fresh names punched into the wood and have a close look at the shafts; the word "Replica" on the new shaft can be replaced by an old shortened driver or spoon shaft. Beware of the lofted clubs of old being converted to water irons and rake irons. Holes and teeth can be put in any part of the blade; then well worn cold chisels can do the rest. It is possible to be fooled! New collectors are also warned about golf ball moulds (they change hands for over £200 now). These moulds, generally smooth or indented inside, are to be found, so have them authenticated, unless bought at a reputable auction house, or from a bona fide dealer.

In conclusion, perchance I should be putting fear into the collector's mind, let me say that I have been referring only to the unscrupulous few; all genuine collectors, dealers and professionals will aid and assist you in your quest for acquiring antiques and curios; it benefits them too even if it is for money or investment. The number of collectors in golf equipment is rapidly growing; many are fanatically enthusiastic, searching far and wide; others plod along in their own locale . . . any one of them may at sometime discover the greatest treasure, it may come via a renowned auction house, it may also be discovered in a dingy little junk shop. May Lady luck smile on you.

15. MARKS & MAKERS

J. McEWAN
1st McEwan stamp

McEWAN

PHILP

COSSAR

CARRICK

JACKSON

MUNRO

PHILIP/FORGAN

TOM MORRIS

WM. PARK

'STRATH

DUNN

R. FORGAN

HUTCHISON

CARRICK

CARRICK

BISHOP & HENDRY
LEITH

R. CONDIE
ST. ANDREWS

W. GIBSON & CO. LTD.
KINGHORN

Harrower
Carnoustie

JN. GRAY

Jn. GRAY
PRESTWICK

MARKS & MAKERS

R. WILSON
MAKER
ST. ANDREWS

ROBERT WHITE
MAKER
ST. ANDREWS

NICOLL
LEVEN
Early Mark

Later Mark
NICOLL
LEVEN

F H AYRES

A & NCSL

ANDERSON
ANSTRUTHER

D. ANDERSON
& SONS
ST. ANDREWS

AAA
ANDERSONS
LONDON

ANDERSON
ANSTRUTHER
AAA

ST. ANDREWS
ANSTRUTHER

Anderson & Gourlay
St. Andrews

MARKS & MAKERS

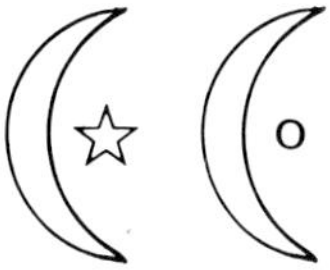

GOURLEY

SPENCE & GOURLEY

C. GIBSON

Urquhart

BG co.

British Golf Co. London Ltd.

A.G. SPALDING
& BROS.

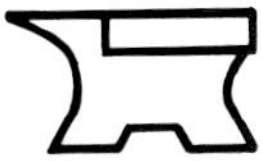

HAMMER FORGED

MARKS & MAKERS

T. MORRIS
ST. ANDREWS

T. Morris Jr.

Pre 1900

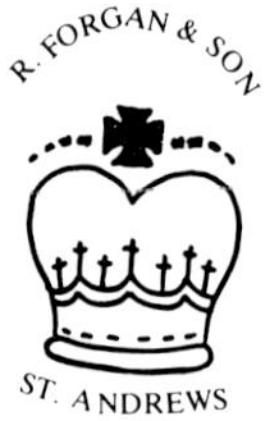

After 1901

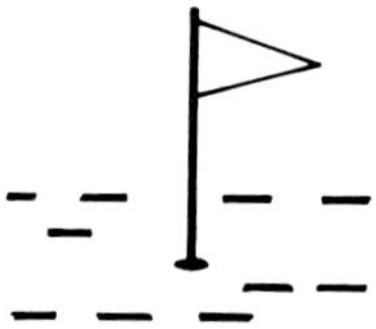

R. FORGAN & SON

T. STEWART
Old Mark

T. S. St. A.
Reg. Trade Mark
New Mark

T. STEWART

T. STEWART

A. FORGAN
GLASGOW

D + W AUCHTERLONIE
ST. ANDREWS

TOM AUCHTERLONIE
& SON

MARKS & MAKERS

ST. ANDREWS
GOLF CO.

ST. ANDREWS GOLF CO.

B • S
A

BRODIE & SONS
ANSTRUTHER

R. CONDIE
ST. ANDREWS

B

BRODIE & CO.
ANSTRUTHER

THE SCOT

NICOLL OF LEVEN

W. GIBSON & CO. LTD
KINGHORN

M. BINGHAM

'CLINGER' MODEL
by Gibson

FIFE
KINGHORN
GOLF CO

T. NICHOLSON

Scott of
Elie (Fife)

MARKS & MAKERS

P G C A
LION BRAND

HAMMER BRAND

Johnstone Bros
Tayport

W. HEWITT
CARNOUSTIE

C. Brand Carnoustie

J. & W. CRAIGIE
CARNOUSTIE

COCHRANE
CARNOUSTIE

T. Harrower
Carnoustie

J. WINTON
MONTROSE

HAND FORGED

MADE IN SCOTLAND

REGD.

GLASGOW GOLF CO.

PREMIER GOLF CO.

MARKS & MAKERS

Cochrane
Edinburgh

STIRLING & GIBSON
CLEEK & IRON MAKERS
JORDAN LANE
EDINBURGH

C. DAVIDSON
MUSSELBURGH

McEWAN
MUSSELBURGH

W. PARK

W. PARK & SON

W. DUNN

later mark of
BISHOP &
HENDRY

HENDRY &
BISHOP

BEN SAYERS
NORTH BERWICK
Old Mark

BEN SAYERS
2nd Mark

STANDARD GOLF CO.
SUNDERLAND

Blackheath Golf Co.
BY SPALDING

F. JOHNSON LTD
LONDON

CLAN

REGD

GOLF CO
LONDON

MARKS & MAKERS

J. B. HALLEY & CO. LTD.

J. B. HALLEY & CO. LTD.

J. B. HALLEY

FLIWEEL
CANN & TAYLOR

Castle Golf Co.

CASTLE GOLF CO.

C. GIBSON
WESTWARD HO

BENETFINK
LONDON

JACK WHITE
LONDON

BY ROLLINS & PARKER

STANDARD GOLF CO
BIRMINGHAM

LEYLAND & BIRMINGHAM
RUBBER CO

LOCKWOOD BROWN
LONDON

MARKS & MAKERS

R S T

Sherlock, Ray & Turner

WELL MADE

WELL MADE

A. PATRICK, LEVEN

GRAMPIAN RANGE
for Turner by W. Gibson

W. Gibson

Northwood
"KNOWN THE WORLD OVER"

P. G. Allday & Co Ltd
Birmingham

COMET BRAND

Craigie of Montrose

Martin &
Martin & Kirkcaldy

F. H. AYRES

PUNCH

G. NICOLL

A. PATRICK OF LEVEN

GLASGOW GOLF CO.

SCOTT OF ELIE

MONOPLANE

MARKS & MAKERS

J. B. HALLEY & CO. LTD.

W. OKE

BY F. H. AYRES

TRULINE

LEYLAND & BIRMINGHAM RUBBER CO

J. Dewsbury & Son
Walsall
Iron-head makers 1909

J. H. Hawkins & Co. Ltd.
Walsall

W. GIBSON
KINGHORN

W. GIBSON
KINGHORN

K

J. ANDERSON, PERTH

Wright & Ditson
BEE LINE
ST. ANDREWS
&
ONTARIO

WRIGHT & DITSON
BRANTFORD & ONTARIO

INDEX

INDEX

INDEX

NAMED MODELS